POWERFUL PROPHETIC WORDS
FROM THE THRONE OF GRACE

From the Potter's Heart

PASTOR/EVANGELIST BARBARA LYNCH

WORDS FROM HER FATHER VOLUME 1

Isaiah 64:8 (NKJV)

"⁸…You *are* our Father, We *are* the clay…"

Contact the Author
Light-Bearer Publishing Company
Attn: Pastor Barbara B. Lynch
1458 Parkers Chapel Road
barbaralynch@lighthousechurchinc.org

ISBN 978-0-9861572-4-0

For Worldwide Distribution, Printed in the U.S.A.

III

IV

CONTENTS

V

INTRODUCTION

There is no greater joy than to hear from the one that you love. Love makes everything work. When you enjoy a relationship with our heavenly Father, He lavishes His love upon you. Many people do not experience love in this earth realm. It is not until they receive salvation that they really begin to understand what love is all about.

This is a collection of the thoughts from the heart of the Potter. The one who made you, the one who breathed life into you. Take these thoughts and use them to grow and become the man or woman that the Potter has created you to be.

Enfolded in these pages are words that are meant to instruct, encourage, lift up and build your faith. These words spring out the relationship of that I have with my heavenly Father. If it were not for Him and His goodness towards me, I would not be here. He has grafted Himself within me and made me His own. From the very beginning of our relationship He has always shared His heart with me.

Sometimes those moments of intimacy created a strong sense of His presence. It is His presence that will sustain you and bring you through the ups and downs of life. You will find folded within these pages strength, hope, and mercy. You will learn how much and to what extent our Father cares for us.

This is the first volume of prophetic utterances that were given from 2003 to 2013. I hope that you enjoy them and are able to grow in your walk with the Father.

Be Ye Holy…

Exodus 19:6 KJV

[6] And ye shall be unto me a kingdom of priests,
and an holy nation...

BE YE HOLY

~~~~~

I am coming to bring My Bride on home. It is time to get your house in order. It is time to cleanse the temples and make them holy. The time has come for My true worshippers to follow Me. It is time to set yourself apart from the cares of this world and come unto Me and worship Me with a pure heart. Worship must come from the heart. Worship must be pure and untouched by the cares of this world.

Holy! Holy! Holy! That is where you should be church. You should be walking **Holy** before a **Holy** God. Your garments should be spotless. You should be a light in a dark, dark place. Come away My beloveds and do the great and mighty works that I have called you forth to do. No longer, be stuck in the quagmire of filth that the world wallows in. Stand firm on a sure foundation and allow My spirit to lead guide and direct your very footsteps.

Step aside and allow My **Holy** Angels access into your lives. Allow My angelic host to fight your battles for you as you go forth to conquer the enemy in others lives. Know this day that I have your back church and the enemy has no strength as you stand in My presence and become Holy vessels of honor.

~~~~~

Tell My people that this is the way it is. There is no other God before them. If they are truly mine, All other gods must go. If truth is to be revealed in its fullness, I will be their only God. All other gods must go. Procrastination is a terrible word. It holds so many captive at this given hour. Tomorrow is all that I hear in their prayer closets. They do not understand what I am all about. They think I am some foreign object that has no power nor authority. But they will all soon see who I realy am.

Take your helmet of salvation and go forth with the sword of the spirit and your shield of faith and conquer the enemy on every side. They will come from the north, south, east and west, but they can by no means harm My true children of the hour.

Woe! Woe unto all the Scribes and Pharisees for I am coming after them and I will destroy all their dead works. The enemy has used them to destroy My camps all across this earth, but now the tide has turned and I will destroy their camps. I am **holy** and all who follow after Me and declare My name shall also be **holy** as I am **holy**.

Matthew 23:13-39 NKJV [13] "But woe to you, scribes and Pharisees, hypocrites! For you shut up the kingdom of heaven against men; for you neither go in *yourselves,* nor do you allow those who are entering to go in. [14] Woe to you, scribes and Pharisees, hypocrites! For you devour widows' houses, and for a pretense make long prayers. Therefore you will receive greater condemnation.

[15] "Woe to you, scribes and Pharisees, hypocrites! For you travel land and sea to win one proselyte, and when he is won, you make him twice as much a son of hell as yourselves.

[16] "Woe to you, blind guides, who say, 'Whoever swears by the temple, it is nothing; but whoever swears by the gold of the temple, he is obliged *to perform it.*' [17] Fools and blind! For which is greater, the gold or the temple that sanctifies the gold? [18] And, 'Whoever swears by the altar, it is nothing; but whoever swears by the gift that is on it, he is obliged *to perform it.*' [19] Fools and blind! For which is greater, the gift or the altar that sanctifies the gift? [20] Therefore he who swears by the altar, swears by it and by all things on it. [21] He who swears by the temple, swears by it and by Him who dwells in it. [22] And he who swears by heaven, swears by the throne of God and by Him who sits on it.

[23] "Woe to you, scribes and Pharisees, hypocrites! For you pay tithe of mint and anise and cummin, and have neglected the weightier *matters* of the law: justice and mercy and faith. These you ought to have done, without leaving the others undone. [24] Blind guides, who strain out a gnat and swallow a camel!

[25] "Woe to you, scribes and Pharisees, hypocrites! For you cleanse the outside of the cup and dish, but inside they are full of extortion and self-indulgence. [26] Blind Pharisee, first cleanse the inside of the cup and dish, that the outside of them may be clean also.

[27] "Woe to you, scribes and Pharisees, hypocrites! For you are like whitewashed tombs which indeed appear beautiful

outwardly, but inside are full of dead *men's* bones and all uncleanness. [28] Even so you also outwardly appear righteous to men, but inside you are full of hypocrisy and lawlessness.

[29] "Woe to you, scribes and Pharisees, hypocrites! Because you build the tombs of the prophets and adorn the monuments of the righteous, [30] and say, 'If we had lived in the days of our fathers, we would not have been partakers with them in the blood of the prophets.'

[31] "Therefore you are witnesses against yourselves that you are sons of those who murdered the prophets. [32] Fill up, then, the measure of your fathers' *guilt.* [33] Serpents, brood of vipers! How can you escape the condemnation of hell? [34] Therefore, indeed, I send you prophets, wise men, and scribes: *some* of them you will kill and crucify, and *some* of them you will scourge in your synagogues and persecute from city to city, [35] that on you may come all the righteous blood shed on the earth, from the blood of righteous Abel to the blood of Zechariah, son of Berechiah, whom you murdered between the temple and the altar. [36] Assuredly, I say to you, all these things will come upon this generation.

[37] "O Jerusalem, Jerusalem, the one who kills the prophets and stones those who are sent to her! How often I wanted to gather your children together, as a hen gathers her chicks under *her* wings, but you were not willing! [38] See! Your house is left to you desolate; [39] for I say to you, you shall see Me no more till you say, 'Blessed *is* He who comes in the name of the LORD!' "

~~~~~

My children must get totally and completely out of sin. It is the Adamic sin nature that keeps them in bondage and out of the blessings. I have tried to convey this message to My children over and over again in so many different ways, but they do not grasp the completeness of My message. Why do My children think they can dabble in sin and still be blessed? Every time a mess occurs in My children's lives, they need to immediately check out their walk. Some where along the line they have gotten out of step with Me. It could be in any area. But I want to say at this point, that My children are dabbling in little sins that are killing them both spiritually and financially.

When they decide to walk the **Holy** Walk, then and only then will I bless totally and completely. The eyes must be cleansed and then the whole Body will be cleansed. When My Body quits playing games, then and only then will they receive all the blessings of Abraham, Isaac and Jacob.

~~~~~

I am the way, the truth and the light. All must come to Me for their salvation. There is no other way into the Kingdom. Many are trying to go through other doors to receive their salvation, and it is not going to work. My Son shed His blood at Calvary for all. My Word gives the truth, but the peoples try to pervert My Word and try to make it fit their situations, but that is not going to work.

Complete **Holiness** is where I am at. I know that there are those that are truly trying to become **Holy** and it is those that I am going to pour My Glory into and they shall be freed in an instant, in a twinkling of an eye. I am Just and I am **Holy** and I will in no wise cast out anybody that comes to me in complete repentance.

My people must understand that the enemy is on the prowl. The antichrists have already come upon the scene and also the false prophets. Daughter, it is perilous times that you are living in and My people must be forewarned about the dangers of following false teachers. Listening to false prophets and allowing the antichrist to have dominion over their souls.

Be on the alert peoples! Be on alert for the enemy is prowling about seeking whom he may devour at this given time. Sad to say, but the enemy has infiltrated the church and is taking out My people daily through deception and alluring devices.

Much sorrow is coming upon My peoples because they are giving into seducing spirits and they are believing the lie and abandoning the truth of My Word.

John 14:6 NKJV Jesus said to him, "I am the way, the truth, and the life. No one comes to the Father except through Me.

II Corinthians 7:1 NKJV Therefore, having these promises, beloved, let us cleanse ourselves from all filthiness of the flesh and spirit, perfecting holiness in the fear of God.

Hebrews 12:14 NKJV Pursue peace with all men, and holiness, without which no one will see the Lord:

John 6:37 NKJV All that the Father gives Me will come to Me, and the one who comes to Me I will by no means cast out.

Matthew 24:11 NKJV Then many false prophets will rise up and deceive many.

Matthew 24:24 NKJV For false christs and false prophets will arise and show great signs and wonders, so as to deceive, if possible, even the elect.

II Peter 2:1 NKJV But there were also false prophets among the people, even as there will be false teachers among you, who will secretly bring in destructive heresies, even denying the Lord who bought them, and bring on themselves swift destruction.

I John 4:1 NKJV Beloved, do not believe every spirit, but test the spirits, whether they are of God; because many false prophets have gone out into the world.

II Timothy 3:1 NKJV But know this, that in the last days perilous times will come:

I Peter 5:8 NKJV Be sober, be vigilant; because your adversary the devil walks about like a roaring lion, seeking whom he may devour.

Mark 13:8 NKJV "For nation will rise against nation, and kingdom against kingdom. And there will be earthquakes in various places, and there will be famines and troubles. These are the beginnings of sorrows.

Matthews 24:8 NKJV All these are the beginning of sorrows

I Timothy 4:1 NKJV Now the Spirit expressly says that in latter times some will depart from the faith, giving heed to deceiving spirits and doctrines of demons.

II Thessalonians 2:9-12 NKJV The coming of the
lawless one is according to the working of Satan, with all
power, signs, and lying wonders, and with all unrighteous
deception among those who perish, because they did not
receive the love of the truth, that they might be saved. And
for this reason God will send them strong delusion, that
they should believe the lie, that they all may be
condemned who did not believe the truth but had pleasure
in unrighteousness.

~~~~~

You are dealing with a very angry God. Why should I bless
those who have cursed My Son and Myself and My Holy Spirit over
and over again? They have tread on the precious blood of My one and
only son Jesus. They have defiled the land over and over again. They
have overstepped their jurisdiction and this is the result of total
disobedience and departure from the True and Living God.

After all, I am the creator of all heaven and earth. It is I the
Lord thy God that has sustained this nation up until now. The present
status of this nation is the result of the departure from the True and
Living God and the truths that this nation was founded upon.

Here am I standing at the door and knocking and nobody will
open the door, not even a crack and then they cry out; where is the
God of Abraham, Isaac and Jacob. The answer is: I am where I have
always been, high and lifted up and My Train does fill the temple. The
temple of God has been defiled to the place of being unrecognized any
longer by the church or the world. What did you expect me to do?

To continue to set calmly by and allow all this degradation to
continue?

Whoa! What kind of God do you think that I am? I am a just God and I will not allow the iniquities to continue on any longer. Yes, prophetic words that were spoken in My word are being fulfilled right before your very eyes; because I knew this would all be happening and I knew that there would be a generation of people that would totally turn their eyes off of the True and **Holy** Father.

But I also knew that there would be a remnant of those peoples that would not defile the **Holy** Temple and they would obey the voice of their Father and they would stand up and fight for what is right no matter what the consequences were. And I have found that remnant and they are marching forth right now and they are going to bring **Holiness** back into the temple and they are going to speak righteousness at all cost and they shall bring the Kingdom of Heaven down to earth and all will see that there is a triune God and they will bow their knees before the heavenly throne and they will come full circle around and they will combat the enemy and they will take all the spoils from him.

~~~~~

Tell my church that it is open season on the adversary. Take him out any way you can. Use all the weapons of warfare that I have given you church and blow the enemy out of the waters. Place him under your feet and do not hesitate to let him know that you are a child of the king and he must bow his knee at the sound of the name of Jesus.

Come on church rise up and ride hard and win every battle. King David knew his enemy and he knew his Heavenly Father and there wasn't any battle he was afraid to fight and he always went to battle with the mind of Christ to win at all cost and win he did.

I am calling forth My Bride this morning to come and ride with me and defeat the enemies of darkness with one final blow of **holiness** and total concentration unto the Most High God. As you place yourself into the army of the Lord, you will become more than a conqueror through My son. Rise up in battle and fight the good fight of faith and know that the enemy has already lost ground. Read my word it is full of the prophetic things that will occur before the end and if you read the word diligently, you will see that you have already won without lifting up a finger.

Blow the trumpet of victory and then march onto Glory. Blow the trumpet loud and clear so the enemy's ears will ring with the sound of triumph. Come My Mighty Army March.

March. March and keep on marching right on up into Glory. For it is in My Glory that all things are accomplished. It is as My Light shines upon you that you will be changed from Glory to Glory.

Oh how I wish that each and every one of you would submit all of yourself unto the voice of the Most High God and receive instruction and then go forth into total victory.

I tell you that My Church shall walk in total victory even in the midst of the strongest storm.

And believe me strong storms will cover this entire earth but My Glory shall shine through them all.

~~~~~

My people are in for one of the biggest miracles of their lives. They are going to move from Glory to Glory and great signs and wonders will follow. The book of Acts will be seen all over again along with the Book of Joel.

It is resurrection time once again. It is time to step out of the mundane and step into the glorious reality of what I am all about. Yes, darkness is going to cover this earth, but am I not the true light? Did I not give a promise that when the gross darkness comes, that My light would shine through the darkness? Then church arise and fulfill My Word. Do the works of My Son Jesus and then do the greater works.

Do not switch back and forth from doubt and belief. Believe My Word and stay there and then accomplish all that My Word tells you that you can accomplish. My Glory Cloud is here. It is here to manifest My Glory in all its fullness. Will you be one of those who carry My Glory in truth, righteousness and **Holiness**?

Come away My beloved ones. Even this day come away with Me into the heavenly realm where My Glory prevails for all to see. Come up higher and stay and commune with Me in truth and holiness. Seek Me with all your heart and you shall surely find Me.

Always remember that I am an all consuming God and I want to consume My peoples totally and completely with My Glory so that all will know that you have stood in the presence of the King of Kings and Lord of Lords.

~~~~~

The church shall stand on her own two feet at this given time. She will no longer rely on the world system to keep her afloat. It is resurrection time and I am resurrecting my church to go forward in the spirit and accomplish the mighty works that I have called her forth to accomplish.

The way is made straight before My church's feet. She will not stumble and fall this time. She will come forth conquering on all sides, for the worldly system is falling and will not influence My Church any longer.

Take up the sword and follow Me church, for we are on a mission to set the captives free and deliver all from bondage that have been bound low all these many years by the adversary. You shall have power and authority from on high and you shall go forth conquering on all sides.

I have spoken of this day in Joel and it has come upon the scene and this is the time for total victory on all sides. Arise and Shine for your light has come.

Arise church! Arise as more than conquerors and take up the banner of **holiness** and march to the drum beat of the Holy Spirit and conquer. As David conquered his enemies, you shall also conquer the enemies that are on the forefront.

~~~~~

Tell My people to let it all go. Tell my people it is time to step out into the supernatural. Tell My people that life as it is, is not worth living, but as they let it all go, I will transport them into the supernatural and then the mundane things of this world will quickly fade away and they will climb upon the lap of their Father and they shall see the Glory Cloud descend upon them and they shall see every need met according to My Riches in Glory. It is time little ones, to quit allowing the wiles of the evil one to torment your minds. It is time to place him under your feet and crush him once and for all. It is time to raise the banner of victory and keep it raised high. For as you go forth, the enemy will tremble and the enemy will flee on every side, for My Holy Angels that have been given charge over thee will stand in full authority by your side and break the enemy's hold over your life.

It is time little ones to ascend the hill of **holiness** where the enemy cannot reach you and it is time to come into the fullness of the supernatural and allow Me the privilege of leading you by the still waters even though the tempest winds blow all around about thee. IT IS TIME!

The fullness of time has come. The fullness of time is here, just walk ye there in it, saith the Father.

I heard the Lord say: "As it was in the days of Noah so it is right now." This hour the floods are coming as they eat, drink and marry.

"As it was in Sodom and Gomorrah so it is right now." The fires are coming and destroying as they did in Sodom and Gomorrah.

When God was ready to destroy Sodom and Gomorrah He sent an angel to warn (Lot and only Lot) to flee the City.

But today prophecy has been going forth, to the entire body of Christ about the destruction that is coming upon America, but who is truly listening?

Our Father has given us warning after warning, but we are not heeding those warnings.

It is time for the Body of Christ to prepare themselves totally and completely for the soon return of our Lord Jesus Christ.

It is time for complete **holiness.** It is time to take up our cross and follow Him daily.

OVERLAP HOLY/LOVE/FORGIVE

~~~~~

Turn the other cheek! It is (turn the other cheek time. For my people to walk with me the entire way; they must learn to turn the other cheek and quit destroying one another at every turn.

What about **Love?** What about **forgiveness?** What about helping a brother in need? What about Jesus?

My people, look not to My hand for provision when you are so busy destroying your brother and your sister. I am a God of Love and Peace. I am a God of Grace and Compassion.

Those who call themselves mine should be walking the same path My son walked oh so many years ago. He is sitting in the heavenlies with Me right now forever interceding for you.

Come out from among the world little ones. Stop being one of the world and turn around and face Me with a determination that you will die out to self and you will be just like My Son Jesus and you will walk the same path He walked without grumbling and complaining.

Take your stance with Me little ones and never be moved from your foundation. I am the great I am and I will never fail you. This is a promise from your Heavenly Father who sees all and knows all and is telling His little ones that they must turn and face Kingdom principles and **come out from among them and be ye clean** who bear the vessel of the Lord.

> **Matthew 5:39 NKJV** "But I tell you not to resist an evil person. But whoever slaps you on your right cheek, turn the other to him also.

> **Luke 6: 29 NKJV** "To him who strikes you on the one cheek, offer the other also. And from him who takes away your cloak, do not withhold your tunic either.

> **Luke 6: 35 – 36 NKJV** "But love your enemies, do good, and lend, hoping for nothing in return; and your reward will be great, and you will be sons of the Highest. For He

is kind to the unthankful and evil. [36.]"Therefore be merciful, just as your Father also is merciful.

Isaiah 52:11 NKJV Depart! Depart! Go out from there, touch no unclean thing; go out from the midst of her, be clean, you who bear the vessels of the Lord.

II Corinthians 6:16 – 18 NKJV "…For you are the temple of the living God. As God has said: "I will dwell in them and walk among them. I will be their God, and they shall be My people. [17.]Therefore "Come out from among them and be separate, says the Lord. Do not touch what is unclean, and I will receive you." [18.]I will be a Father to you, and you shall be My sons and daughters, says the Lord Almighty."

OVERLAP HOLY/WORSHIP

~~~~~

Follow your heart in all things, for I am in the heart. I am leading My people down a path of great adventures and they will once again understand that I truly am Lord of this nation. They will understand that I do things in My timing and not theirs. I have not missed anything. After all, am I not the creator of all things? Therefore, I know the perfect timing of all things.

Daughter, tell My peoples to look up, for their redemption doth draweth nigh. I am their redemption and I am coming in a Great Cloud of Glory. But before that eventful day occurs, there is so much work to be done here on this earth for My Kingdom. Many souls to be brought into the Kingdom. Many have not even heard the gospel of Jesus Christ. Many have not had the opportunity to receive My Son into their bosoms. So many souls hanging in the balance and no one to speak the truth to them; to allow them to decide their fate. I want every man to have the opportunity to receive My Son or reject Him. I want no one to perish. I am making a way for the Word to go forth, and I need dedicated committed servants to go forth with this gospel that saves the souls from eternal damnation.

Rise up peoples of this nation and tune your ears to My voice, for I am speaking volumes, but not many are listening. I am calling from the four corners of this earth, calling all who will heed the sound of My voice.

So much idolatry out there. So much walking in the flesh, leaving My Holy Spirit out of their lives and then blaming Me when all things tumble around about them.

Hold up **Holy** hands and **worship** Me with a pure heart and then I will come and sup with you. Then I will speak softly into your ears the plans that I have for this nation. Plans that will edify and lift up. Plans to bring this nation to her knees and then rise her back up again.

Come My **Holy** Vessels. Come unto Me with pure hearts; pure motives and pure hands and I will send you to the nations with a Right Now Word to give to My people who sit in My houses all over this nation and are perishing.

OVERLAP HOLY/TOTAL LOVE

~~~~~

Where are you going church? That is a question you must ask yourself and come to a final decision of where you want to end up.

I want you in My glory realm; but where do you want to be?

To be in My glory realm you must be walking in total **holiness,** purity of heart and a **total love** walk. I have given you all that you need to line up with My Word and fulfill the destiny that My church has always been called to fulfill.

Many signs, wonders and miracles will begin to occur when all My Criteria has been met. Are you wondering why you are not seeing My glory in all of its fullness? Well, examine yourself; have you fulfilled My criteria for an all-out glory drop?

I am going from town to town; city to city looking for churches that have fulfilled the criteria that I have placed before My church; but I am finding very few that have yielded themselves totally and completely to My calling. WILL YOU BE ONE OF THOSE THAT I CAN USE?

That is My question to you in this strategic hour.

Come and Dine...

John 21: 12 KJV

[12] Jesus saith unto them, Come and dine...

COME AND DINE…

~~~~~

It is now time to come up out of the wilderness. It is now time to climb up that mountain of total victory. Iron is sharpening iron at this given time and I am doing a great and powerful works amongst My people. It is important that My people have their ears yielded to My voice, for I am giving clear cut directions at this given time and it will take you over the top and it will lower My Glory Cloud so that you walk in continual blessings. Come away My beloved ones. Come away and dine at the table that I have spread out before you. Come I say, Come away with Me to the secret place of the most high God. **Come and dine.**

~~~~~

2009 will be a year of rejoicing and a year of mourning. Many things will occur that will either cause my people to rejoice or they will cause my people to mourn.

I have been calling my true church unto myself, but not many have come. Not many are listening.

22

Daughter, they must rise up above this mess that has come upon this land.

They can no longer linger around the cesspool of sin and degradation that has overcome the world. My church must separate herself from the mundane things of this earth and they must come up hither and they must commune with the Most High God. I am truly their father and I truly want them to sit at my feet and partake of my nature. I want them to know me intimately. I want them to come to the foot of the cross daily and commune with me, not just once and awhile.

Some have lost their first love and they must return unto their first love before they can cross over Jordan with me and my angelic host of warriors. I have truly encompassed my true church with my angelic host and that host will bring them through all the storms that life throws at them.

Take my hand this night church and lean not to your own understanding, but stand like you have never stood before and allow me to be your all and all. For I know what you have need of. I know what the enemy has planned for your life. I am your sufficiency. I will supply saith the father. Just trust me in all areas of your life. If you trust me in one area, you must trust me in all areas.

Come now; let us dine together this night, for I have a banquet spread out before you. Come and dine little ones, come and dine at the Father's table. There is plenty for all.

~~~~~

Little one; little does the church understand what I am about to do within My walls. What I do within my walls will filter out into the streets and many salvations will occur. Who can tell what I will do? Absolutely no one! I am the only one that knows what is going to happen and when it will happen. Take My Word to the streets church; take My Word to the streets. For it is time for the Word to be heard on the street corners of this earth. Think it not strange what you are about to see and hear. Think it not strange what you are about to experience. Come Church; come up higher in Me this night and sup at My Table that I have spread before you. I have been calling a long time for My church to come and dine but as of this date they have not accepted the invitation. How I desire to sup with My people; but if they won't come, I will go into the streets and compel them to come in; and they will come and they will sup and they will glean much from My Kingdom.

IT IS STREET EVANGELISM TIME!

GET PREPARED, FOR YOU WILL GO TO THE STREETS AND YOU WILL SEE MANY SALVATIONS THE WORLD IS READY FOR MY SON AND I AM TAKING MY SON TO THEM AT THIS GIVEN TIME

STREET EVANGELISM IS THE THEME FROM THIS POINT ON

TAKE ME TO THE STREETS OF ALL THE NATIONS

AND JUST WATCH WHAT I WILL DO. THE FOUR WALLS DO NOT WANT ME, BUT THE MARKET PLACES DO.

MY WIND IS IN THE AIR AND WHEN YOU GO FORTH, IT WILL BE MY WIND THAT IS BLOWING THAT WILL BLOW ACROSS THE HEARTS OF THE SINNERS AND COMPEL THEM TO **COME AND DINE.**

Matthew 22:8-10 "Then he said to his servants, `The wedding is ready, but those who were invited were not worthy. [9.]Therefore go into the highways, and as many as you find, invite to the wedding. [10.]So those servants went out into the highways and gathered together all whom they found, both bad and good. And the wedding hall was filled with guests.

~~~~~

Repent for this nation little one. Be in constant prayer and intercession for this nation and its lost and dying peoples. I am a God of Justice and I am bringing justice in the middle of the storms of life. I am fulfilling all the prophetic words that are written in My Word at this given time and I am fulfilling the desires of the people's hearts. They wanted a king, I gave them a king. They wanted abundance without sacrifice; I gave them abundance. They wanted and they wanted and they wanted. I allowed their wants to be met, but now I am turning the tide and now **I want**.

I want their full undivided attention.

I want complete repentance for the turmoil in this land.

I want repentance on all fronts.

I want My children to come back home where they belong; where I can bless them and where I can give them the overflow that they need.

Beloved ones come and dine at the King's table once again. Bring Me into the spotlight. Allow Me room in your hearts once again, for I desire to bless this generation of people's like no other generation has been blessed. This is a new era; a new dawning and My Glory is about to cover this earth in an unprecedented way. Come My Beloved ones. **Come** to the King's table and **dine** and be filled.

~~~~~

Paul said: I beseech you my brethren that above all things, have faith in your father. I say unto My people this day: "Have faith in your Father, the Father of Abraham, Isaac and Jacob. The same Father that created all things, both the heaven and the earth and every living creature."

My will is that all be blessed and that all prosper, even as their souls prosper.

My will is that My children walk in complete obedience to My very Word and lean not to their own understanding.

My will is that each of My children obtain the riches of heaven that I speak of so often in My Word.

I desire that each of My children walk under the umbrella of blessings that I have for them.

My desire is that My children stop the fowler from stealing from them.

I am on the move and I desire that My children move with Me. There is absolutely nothing to stop My children, except their doubt and unbelief. I have supplied them with everything they need to advance in My Kingdom.

Now is the Time. Now is the time of great salvations upon this earth. Now is the time of the moving of the mighty rushing waters that I have spoke about in times past. Now! Now! Now is the acceptable time.

Come and dine! That has been My invitation to My children for years now. And I am calling once again (come and dine) for The Master truly is calling for His bride to come and dine in the great banquet hall that I have prepared for this grand occasion.

Come little ones. **Come and dine** and eat until you are full to over flowing. This is overflow time for My Body.

Scripture reference: Ephesians 4

~~~~~

Tell My people that I have come for them. Tell them that I have a very special purpose for coming at this specific timeframe in their walk with Me. This is the set hour and this is the set day for their divine visitation.

Tell them that this month will be a pivotal point in their lives. A pivotal point that will change them forever into the image of My Precious Son Jesus; for I have come in all My Fullness and I plan on consuming My children with this fullness and I will leave no stone unturned; for I am truly with them to do and accomplish all that I have foreordained to accomplish.

This is resurrection month. This is transforming month; This is the month of the turtle dove wooing his bride. This is the month spoken of in the book of Joel.

All that survived the terrible onslaught of the wicked evil one is now ready to come up into the open heaven that is over them and prepare themselves to dine with Me continually.

Come and Dine!

Grace...

John 1: 17 KJV

[17] For the law was given by Moses, but grace and truth came by Jesus Christ...

GRACE

~~~~~

Little one, the cares of this world are taking My church under. They are placing their eyes on the circumstances of life that are surrounding them and they are dying minute by minute. Have I not spoken and have I not said that I am with My children? Have I not said that no weapon formed against them shall ever prosper? I have spoken and what I have spoken is truth. What the enemy speaks and portrays is a lie. In fact, it is a bold faced lie. I am not a man that I should lie and I am in total control of all things and I have brought My children up out of the land of Egypt, out of bondage into the marvelous light of My Beloved Son. I AM restoring all that the canker and palmer worm has stolen.

The problem here is that I am working on My Time Table and not theirs. I am working everything out in perfect timing. Why will My Church not see this? Why do they go about yielding their minds to the darkness? Why are they **not** listening to My still small voice that is trying to lead, guide and direct them? There are so many WHYS in the atmosphere right now. There is **no** praising Me! And that is what I have required of My Church, total praise, total worship, unhindered with Doubt and Unbelief, just total praise and worship.

Church, seek for the Joy of the Lord, for that is where your strength comes from. I am well able to accomplish all that I have begun. Have I not started a good works in you? Then I AM able to accomplish all that I start.

Come away My Beloved into that secret place with Me and allow Me to breathe upon you fresh new wind. A wind that will restore and a wind that will usher you into the Throne Room of **grace** and you will begin to understand that My **grace** is truly sufficient.

~~~~~

Nowhere in My Word does it say Failure! But My people use that word always. I never geared My children to failure. The enemy has come in and accused My people falsely and they have now branded themselves as failures.

My Word is all positive about what I want to do with My People. My Word tells you over and over again about My **grace** and mercy. If you have failed, repent and come on and do the mighty works I have foreordained you to accomplish in this life time. The hour truly is late and the workers at this given time are so few. Take up your sword and follow Me and accomplish all that I have laid out before you in this dispensation. It still is and has always been: Line upon line and precept upon precept. Here a little and there a little. You do not see the grand picture, but you will as you focus your attention on the things that I am calling you to do, instead of your petty failures.

Abraham was a man of total faith and he accomplished all that I called him forth to do. Even though great obstacles were placed in his path over and over again, his faith did not falter. He stepped through each and every door that was opened unto him. I am asking each of you to do the same. At no time did I ever leave or forsake Abraham. He was a Father of many nations. I sustained him through every trial that came his way. He knew from whence he came and he knew where he was going.

Stay firmly rooted and grounded in Me at this given time, for I am taking My peoples on a grand tour of the heavenly realm and you shall see all of My splendor. Always remember I am a God of the impossibles and My arm is not short. Think big and come after all the promises I have given you.

~~~~~

My people are perishing for lack of knowledge. And My children I have been giving you fresh manna from heaven and I want you to take that fresh manna from heaven to the people who are perishing, but My children you can't take that fresh manna, because you keep losing it. The enemy keeps stealing it from you. It never gets rooted. It never gets grounded. It goes in and back out again and I am calling you forth this night to let My word go deep into your bosom. Let it go deep into your bosom and take root. It has to first of all take root within you and then you will be able to take it to the people that are perishing. I am the husbandman and I prune My vineyard so that there is good fruit. But My children I have been pruning and I have been pruning and I have been pruning it and the fruit is still not bearing. And I say unto you this day: the Word says the last enemy to defeat is death. And that is death to your flesh. Death to your fleshly desires. This is the reason why your fruit will not come to fruition. It is because you still give into your fleshly desires. You must die to your flesh. You must die to your own desires. And desire to only do what I am calling you forth to do.

My children I will feed you fresh manna from heaven and I never break my promises because my promises are covenants. And I do not break a covenant. You break the covenant not Me. And I am calling each one of you in here this night to die out to your flesh. I am asking each one of you in here this night to come up higher with Me, I say come hither even this night. And come sit at the throne of grace and sit at My feet and allow Me to feed you fresh manna from heaven.

The hour is soon coming upon this land where many will perish. Much fear will strike the peoples there will be much running to and fro. Many will be worried. Many will be concerned. Many will even die. And I say that you have the Word, you just do not water it. You do not cause it to grow. I am saying get into My Word, get into My Word. Your spirit is starved for My Word. Get into my Word. I want to mature the word you already have in you. But you place your mind upon your problems. You do not place your mind upon Me the Living God. Trust in Me My children, trust in Me, I am able to do all that I have promised to do.

You must die out to your flesh! You must! You must do this or your flesh will kill you, spiritually and physically. I am calling each one of you to climb higher this night and you do that by dying out to your flesh. I am in your midst even as I speak. I am in your midst and I am walking to and fro. And I am looking and I am saying you are starved! You are starved! You are starved. The Word is not growing inside of you. It goes in your head and out your ears. I want it to go into your Spirit man. And I want you to use My Word to set the other captives free.

Others of you in here, the only time you call on Me is when you need Me, you never fellowship with Me otherwise. And I am calling you to fellowship with Me all the time. I am asking you to come to the throne of **grace** and sit in My presence and talk to Me. Just sit down and talk to Me. You don't have to get all spiritual! Just talk to Me. You can tell Me your troubles. I don't mind that. You can talk to Me about your worldly affairs, I don't mind that. But I desire for you to talk to Me. You need to spend time communing with Me.

And those of you who are running from Me, I expect you to stop. And I expect you to turn around and face Me squarely. Repent and come on and do the works I have called you forth to do. For the hour truly is late! The hour truly is late! And many are perishing. Many are perishing for lack of knowledge and you have the knowledge hidden down in your bosom. You refuse to give it forth. You refuse to repent and come full circle around and serve Me with all of your heart. You will be held accountable for those souls that are dying daily because you refuse to repent and follow Me.

~~~~~

The main stream is full of defilement and I must cut off the heads to preserve the body. I am a just and true God and I must bring My axe down upon My houses, if the world is going to be able to trust Me. The defilement in the church has run rampant for far too long now. I must take action upon those in Leadership positions, whether they like it or not. I have sent My **grace** ahead of Me for them to repent, but not so. Why would the world want to come into pollution? They live in pollution in the world. They are looking for security, some sense of peace and conformity. They don't need more confusion.

I drew the line in the sand two years ago and I have been working on My leaders since that time, but to no avail. Now judgment has come to the house of the Lord. Jeremiah saw the judgment and he lamented and cried out to Me, but the peoples would not change. You are living in the same hour.

~~~~~

There are mountains and then there ARE MOUNTAINS! I

am calling you forth at this given time to hurdle over the mountain tops and stay securely rooted and grounded in Me. I know who I am, but My people do not know who they are and the enemy comes again and again to steal from My chosen people. When will they learn? How long will it take? For some it will take so long that it will be to late. For others they are going to wise up quickly and they will arise out of the ash heap and serve Me with all of their hearts. This is the greatest time of decision in the church history. This decision will make or break My church. It is time to arise up out of the ash heap and serve the Living God and serve Him only, for I will have no other Gods before Me. I am true and I am faithful and I fail not My peoples. Look up peoples! Look up, for your redemption doth truly draw nigh.

Just as quickly as New Orleans was destroyed, I will devastate this whole earth. Many will be running to and fro. The peoples will be about their normal everyday lives and suddenly out of nowhere I will appear and it will be all over. I have spoken this before and nobody heeded My voice. I am speaking it again and still they will not heed My voice. Destruction must come upon this nation, for they are making themselves a nation without a Father. They are taking Me out of everything and I am wroth with My peoples. Come and take council from Me, saith the Father. Come and take council from Me and learn the truth of what is happening round about you. You are transgressing My laws daily and I will not permit it any longer. You have cast Me asunder. You have brought Me to shame over and over again. Enough is enough and I am tired of this horseplay that you call church and I have come to put an end to it.

Take not council from the ungodly, for they are alrcady lost. Seek council from Me, for I am your counselor. I and only I have the answers to your questions. Why do you forsake Me over and over again? Why not just come to the throne of **grace** and accept all that

My son did for you? WHY? That is My question to you tonight.
WHY?

~~~~~

My people who are called by name will assemble together at
this given time and they shall receive divine instruction from their
Heavenly Father. They shall come directly to the throne of **grace** and
receive their orders directly from Me, their Father. There will be no
more questions. There will just be instruction. I will lead, guide and
direct My people in the path that they shall go and no more will they be
tossed to and fro. They shall know what it is to be instructed in
holiness and then to walk in holiness. I am with My peoples, I have
not left them nor forsaken them as some have voiced. Oh no, on the
contrary, I have been with them every step of the way and they shall
soon see why they had to go down the path that they journeyed on for
these past several years. Yes, it has been a hard path, but I was there
every step of the way and I did not turn My back on them as some
supposed. Happy are those who trusted in their Father for direction,
for they shall see the salvation of the Lord.

~~~~~

This is just the beginning of sorrows for My people. There is
much destruction on the horizon and My people are not prepared to
meet this destruction. They have prayed and then laid back on their
laurels and believe that nothing is going to happen, but the destruction
is coming upon the land. Life will go on, but not the same as before.
Many will be running to and fro and they will not be able to find peace,
but My true church will know Me as the center of peace and they will
lead the others to the place of peace that only abides within Me. I have
asked My people to come out from under the mundane and walk in the
supernatural, but they are refusing to do so. Time will tell! Time will tell
on those who would not heed My warnings and all will finally see that I

truly did speak and warn My church, but to no avail. The time of great warfare is upon this land and you (church) must war as never before. You must come to the throne of **grace** as never before. You must stay at the altar of incense as never before and you must come out victorious on all sides. I have spoken and so shall it be, saith the Lord.

Warfare! Warfare! Warfare on all sides and only those who have been trained to walk in My circumference of safety will make it through this terrible hour of great warfare that has come upon this land.

Marshall law will now come into effect. You will see destruction on every side. Many suicides will occur at this given time. Many will walk in fear for their very lives. But I have warned and I have warned, but to no avail. Now My true church will emerge upon the scene with signs, wonders and miracles and they shall bring peace in the midst of this chaotic world. Be still and know that I am God and fight the good fight of faith and prevail at all cost.

~~~~~

Tell My people that I am with them, no matter what the circumstance might be. I do not allow them to flounder on that stormy sea. I come to them just as I came to My disciples and I give them comfort and I give them peace.

I am the Father of all peace and I truly give My Beloved Ones rest in the midst of the deepest storm. I am forever with them and I am always undergirding them. Though the winds may blow and the storms may come, I am STILL GOD.

All must understand that I alone have spoken words over their lives and I alone will give them words of comfort. They have no need of other Gods. All they need is the one true God. I am their Father and I will sustain them; if they will only trust Me to the fullest in all things.

They must understand that I am in the little things as well as the big things. I am in the mundane things as well as the very important things. I am continually with them.

They must totally understand that My **grace** is with them at all times and My **grace** is sufficient in all things.

Saving **grace**! Sustaining **grace**!

His **grace** saves you and then His **grace** sustains you in your walk with Him!

Matthew 14:22-32 NKJV [22] Immediately Jesus made His disciples get into the boat and go before Him to the other side, while He sent the multitudes away. [23] And when He had sent the multitudes away, He went up on the mountain by Himself to pray. Now when evening came, He was alone there. [24] But the boat was now in the middle of the sea, tossed by the waves, for the wind was contrary.

[25] Now in the fourth watch of the night Jesus went to them, walking on the sea. [26] And when the disciples saw Him walking on the sea, they were troubled, saying, "It is a ghost!" And they cried out for fear. [27] But immediately Jesus spoke to them, saying, "Be of good cheer! It is I; do not be afraid."

[28] And Peter answered Him and said, "Lord, if it is You, command me to come to You on the water." [29] So He said, "Come." And when Peter had come down out of the boat, he walked on the water to go to Jesus. [30] But when he saw that the wind *was* boisterous, he was afraid; and

beginning to sink he cried out, saying, "Lord, save me!" [31] And immediately Jesus stretched out *His* hand and caught him, and said to him, "O you of little faith, why did you doubt?" [32] And when they got into the boat, the wind ceased.

~~~~~

My people I am looking for a people who will loose the chains of those who are bound and set the captives free. Do not consider your own flesh; for it is but dung in my eyes. Your job is to save the lost at any cost. Never looking at tomorrow; but concentrating on today and keeping your eyes solely upon Me.

Tell my people to let go and let me be the God of their situations. I want to bless and not curse. I want to bring my people to a perfect place of perfect understanding of who I am and what I am about.

This is not about legalism. This is about My **grace** and My mercy being shed abroad all across the land; for surely I am moving amongst my people and surely I will do a perfect works all across this land.

The enemy will infiltrate American soil this Fall and they will do much damage. You will see plagues of all nature all across this land. Great turmoil is upon the horizon and I am about to show myself strong on behalf of the church. The church will shine in the midst of gross darkness and they will do a great and mighty work for the Kingdom of Light.

Many, many souls hanging in the balance. Many, many souls hungry and thirsty and they don't know where to look for their answer; but they will know and they will run to my houses of refuge in the midst of the strongest storms that will rage all across this land.

Hunger and thirst will prevail in the ensuing days. My people need to be ready to feed the hungry and thirsty ones that are in great need. Be prepared church to take on the enemy at every turn. Be prepared for mass deliverances. You will surely bring the souls out of darkness and bring them into the marvelous light of the true Lord Jesus Christ.

Take up your swords and follow me at all cost. Put on the full armor of God and follow Me with all your hearts.

~~~~~

There is coming a time of an even greater shaking to this nation. Many will fall by the wayside during this shaking, never to be reunited to Me again. They have had the privilege of sitting at My feet; of complete restoration; of seeing My gifts in operation; of walking under the anointing and the power of the most high God; but yet they refuse to stay committed to Me, the most sovereign God of the universe.

This is the peak time of anointing for My peoples, if they will discard all the things of this world and just crawl up on My lap and allow daddy to caress them and heal them of all their hurts, disappointments and confusion.

Nobody; absolutely nobody can imagine the move of My spirit at this given time. This is a generation of glory shakers and they shall carry My glory and it shall shake the very foundations of the religious system.

Many are still running to and fro when I have spoken and said: Be still and know that I am God. Be still and allow the salvation of the Lord work on your behalf. Oh, how the mighty do fall, when they transgress My laws. You will see this great awakening in the Fall of this year and you shall see the great turmoil before this year is out; but I will be flowing in My Glory and I will be pouring out blessing after blessing after blessing; for this is also blessing time for all those who have stood tall and firm in their convictions in Me.

Rejoice and again I say rejoice, for the victory is already won and you are walking in the victory realm.

It will be a Holy Ghost invasion all across this nation and many signs wonders and miracles will be seen throughout this land.

Marriages that have been on the brink of disaster will be suddenly restored. And children that have been wayward for years will suddenly walk into the house of the Lord and be revitalized and rejuvenated and they shall perform the arts for Me and great signs and wonders will follow.

The atmosphere in the entire church is being changed even as I speak. My Angelic host is hovering over the services and they are changing the atmosphere for My signs, wonders and miracles to occur. It shall be a miraculous time of intervention in the Spirit realm and many will move to and fro from earth to heaven and bring great revelations from the throne of **grace**.

The fire of the Holy Spirit will be seen upon My peoples and their faces shall shine with My glory as Moses' face shone. This is an unprecedented time in My glory realm and all that enter into this dimension of My glory will never be the same. And they will do great exploits in My name for all the nations to experience.

Such Holiness! Holiness like you have ever imagined before. My true people will consecrate themselves to me and they will walk in complete holiness before the King of Kings and Lord of Lords and all will know that they are My peoples; for wisdom and divine knowledge will flow forth from them and they shall be a sign and a wonder for My Kingdom.

The church is going through a radical change and nobody will recognize the church when I am finished with her. She too will be a sign and a wonder for My Kingdom authority. She will not tolerate baal in her services; she will not allow the enemies of the cross to remain in her presence, but with all authority she will cast them out and they shall be forever burned in the lake of fire. She will have authority to do all things according to My Word. For I have truly given the keys to the kingdom to My true church and she shall unlock the mysteries of heaven with those keys.

Much insight into the spirit realm will start to occur and many will walk where they have never walked before and they shall know that I am the God of this universe and that I fail them not.

Your weapons are not carnal but mighty to the pulling down of strongholds. That is My Word and that is My promise to the end time remnant. Think no more on the beggarly elements of this world for I have called you to be heavenly minded and I want you to live in the heavenlies.

~~~~~

Tell My people that I am coming soon; sooner than they think. I am on My way with a two edged sword and I will separate and I will divide the lands and the peoples. Much devastation coming upon the land, **but** My Glory shall fill the land and there will be great divisions of darkness and light; for I am removing the darkness from My House and I am bringing the LIGHT OF MY GLORY into My House once again. There will be gnashing of teeth, but I have spoken and so shall it be.

MINDSETS: I have spoken to My people and said; allow Me to give you a BRAND NEW MINDSET and they ignored My request. Now, it is too late. They shall stand at the threshold and be found wanting. Peoples are looking for My **Grace** and it has been with them all along; but MY **GRACE** was not sufficient for them, for they kept looking to the dark side of this world for their answers and pleasures.

Some will drink from the bitter cup of sorrow while others will drink of the cup of abundance. For I am coming after a people who are washed white as snow and who are looking for the soon return of My Son. They have been watching, praying, fasting and seeking My Face and they are the ones that will see My Full Glory upon them and they are the ones that I am going to use in this end time dispensation of My Church.

Rejoice little ones; rejoice for the KING OF KINGS is coming and HE is coming as LORD!

~~~~~

As you stand at My door and knock, I will open unto you the mysteries of My Kingdom. I am sitting My Bride apart from the church and I am teaching her the full Glory of My Kingdom principles. My Bride shall be alert; receptive to heavenly teachings and full of wisdom and understanding of the times that lie before her. She shall know My Kingdom like no others. She will not walk in delusion but she shall have her heart and mind stayed upon the Living King and she shall hear His voice and only His voice.

The trumpet will sound and resound throughout this land. All will know the trumpet call of the All Mighty One has sounded in the darkest hours of Church history. Do not be dismayed by what others are saying, for I will instruct you in all your ways and your knowledge will come from the throne of **grace.**

This is not a time of second guessing. This is a time to know who your redeemer is and serve him whole heartedly. Many will be running to and fro looking for the truth but the truth will evade them on all sides, for they have turned their backs on the real truth and have developed itching ears.

But you My Bride you have been preparing yourself for this hour. You stood the test and now you are ready to go forth with Wisdom and Understanding and teach My people the truth of the times without hesitation.

~~~~~

Go to your battle station and prepare for war. It is an all out war against my true saints. This is the time to follow true righteousness at all cost. This is not the time to compromise your standards. Stand tall church. Stand tall for what you believe in. Take care of those things that I have placed in your hands. Never allow the enemy an in road into your life. Secure the battle station and fight. Take up the shield of faith and the sword and go forth and conquer on all sides. Allow no enemy to escape the camp. Destroy all the enemies.

During this time of battle it is essential to take time to fast and pray in order to get direction from the throne of **grace.** I will give you battle plans as you sit at my feet. There shall be nothing that shall befall my true believers that I cannot conquer.

~~~~~

Thus saith the Lord God Almighty, Who was, Who is and Who is to come. I am going forth with or without you. I have spoken of what I want accomplished at this given time and so very few are yielding to My calling. One day you will look up and know that I have departed from you. You will understand that you missed your window of opportunity. I have spoken to My people so many times and I have given them **grace** upon **grace**, but to no avail. Now, I am moving on. I will now go into the highways and the byways and I am compelling them to come in. Then I will use them to accomplish the mighty works that needs to be accomplished in this dispensation of time.

Oh, peoples, if you would only comprehend what I am about to do and even doing this very moment. It is not just going to be one miracle, but a continuing flow of miracles from Wall street on down. I have a perfect plan and that plan has already been put into operation in this universe that you call home. If you would just look beyond your needs and look into the realm of Glory, you would be totally shocked at what you would see. My Holy Angels are standing at attention. They are awaiting their orders to go forth and accomplish My Mighty Miracles. I have been searching and I have been searching for a man or a woman that will get their head out of the doctrines and theology of man long enough for Me to introduce Myself to them as The Great Miracle Worker.

I have only been able to find a few, but with this few I will accomplish all that I have placed My hand to do upon this earth. You hve not seen anything yet. The shaking will conquer the enemy strongholds in the lives of those who have been bound for all these many years. They will be like the woman with the issue of blood. They will finally touch the hem of My Son's garment and they shall be totally healed. It is so imperative that you seek Me with all your hearts, minds, souls and spirits at this given time, for this is the unleashing of My Supernatural Powers upon the church. All who have ears to hear, hearken unto My voice that thunders from My Holy Throne Room

~~~~~

Church, seek not your own understanding at the present time. Lean solely upon Me, the author and finisher of your very life. I have resounded the word FREEDOM throughout the atmosphere and all that can hear that sound will have freedom in this very hour. Much shrapnel is flying around, but those who are in Me will not be touched by the debris that has come forth from the filth of this world and the sins of the church.

I have spoken so often of MY Grace. And My Grace is sufficient, but only to those who are truly abiding under the shadow of the Almighty. I am the maker of all things. I made heaven and earth and all things pertaining there unto. Why do the nations roar? Why do the peoples think I am out of control? Deception! Deception has entered into the church and My people no longer believe in My Word. They believe the lie. And the lie is taking them under. It is all about CONTROL!

Everybody wants to be in control and the truth of the matter is they are out of control at this given time. I have aligned My Words with the Spirit and the Spirit of Holiness is bringing all truth to the light. Only those who have chosen to remain in darkness will never see the truth of the light. But the Holy Ones! The set apart ones! They shall see the complete truth and this truth shall set them free from all bondage.

The tabernacle of David stands in a secure place and My Word stands in a secure place. My Sons blood stands in a secure place. And now My precious Holy Spirit is standing in the secure place to lead guide and direct those who will yield to my calling.

I have foreordained this time in history. Things are going as I planned. Nobody can change My plans. You are truly living in the days of Sodom and Gomorrah when Abraham cried out "If there is ten just persons" You know the story of Sodom and Gomorrah. Well, this time is the continuance of the story.

Fret not for those who will abort My plan. Stay close to Me and hear My heart beat and follow My Commands. I have spoken and so shall it be.

~~~~~

Daughter, there is a mighty move afoot. I am staging the biggest finale that the church has ever seen. I am choosing the players for this play right now. I am choosing those who are committed to Me with all of their being. I will not choose a player that is halfhearted. I know those that are mine and I am giving them their parts to play even as we speak. This is the finale of all finales. Who will partake of this great play? It will surpass anything Hollywood has put on. The world has seen nothing yet. Just you wait and see what I am about to do with and through My true church.

I am saying come away My beloved ones and partake of this great and final play that is already coming together in the heavenlies. Do not think this a light thing that I am doing at this given time.

I have been so gracious to those who love Me and My **grace** shall abound even more widely as the days progress. The show to stop all shows is about to begin. Who will play the major roles?

~~~~~

46

My Body is still not ready for the mighty outpouring of My Glory. They are still playing around with My anointing. I am now ready to lift My hand of **grace**. That little window of opportunity for true repentance is just about to close. When church are you going to repent and come fully unto Me? When are you going to tire of the games you play over and over again? Come higher with Me. Come higher with me and allow My Glory to fill your temples. I am the Almighty Judge. I have already judged My people and have found them wanting. Little by little many are falling away from the faith. Little by little many are being discouraged and losing hope because they have not clung to the cross of the Almighty One. What has happened to the precious blood of My Son? To many it has no value, but I tell you that it is more precious than gold. The Blood that ran down Calvary's hill has all that you will need. Apply the blood and watch the miracles flow. Come higher church! Come higher! Even this very hour I am calling My chosen ones to let go of the beggarly elements of this world and to flow with Me.

~~~~~

The time is coming and now is, when many souls will be lost. I have sent my word to set the captives free, but to no avail. The body has turned their hearts over to the deceiving spirits and they are being eternally lost each and every day. They play church over and over again, when I have called them to true repentance. They have not heeded My call to true repentance. They have not come under the umbrella of protection that I have provided for them. They will not take heed to the prophets that I have sent their way. They are in the deepest deception known to mankind. What can the holy angels do that have been sent forth to bring total salvation to their souls? Absolutely nothing, for they will not repent. They will not turn from their wicked evil ways. **Grace** has been granted to all, but not all took that grace and allowed it to set them free. How foolish. Oh foolish galatians who has deceived you in this great hour of deliverance? Who has come in like a flood and told you you did not have to heed my warnings. Oh foolish Galatians, you have been completely deceived by the evil one and there is no turning back. I am doing a complete purging and you shall see me purge the threshing floor of all impurities. I have spoken-no-I have thundered and so it shall be.

> **Galatians 3:1-4 NKJV 3** o foolish galatians! Who has bewitched you that you should not obey the truth, before whose eyes jesus christ was clearly portrayed among you as crucified? **2** this only I want to learn from you: did you receive the spirit by the works of the law, or by the hearing of faith? **3** are you so foolish? Having begun in the spirit, are you now being made perfect by the flesh? **4** have you suffered so many things in vain—if indeed *it was* in vain?

~~~~~

As for me and my house we shall serve the Lord. Thus Joshua made this proclamation to all the land. Where oh where are my people who will proclaim the very same words. Daughters of Zion look up into the heavenly realm and choose Me this day. Choose to serve Me with all of thine hearts and lean not upon your own understanding. I Am that I Am and there is none other like unto Me. Why not choose the vessel of honor? Why not come up on the mountain top and abide under the shadow of the Almighty. I am from everlasting to everlasting and I fail you not. I have chosen a peculiar people to sit at My throne room of judgment and to judge this whole earth. Come away My beloved ones and sit in the throne room of **grace** that I may instruct you on judgment. For there are so many false judges upon this land. Fury after fury will be released, but in all this fury, you will see righteous judgments coming forth. I have spoken it and it shall be saith the Almighty One that controls heaven and earth. Am I not the Great

Redeemer? Have I not spoken all things into existence? Yes! And I have not changed; not by one mite have I Changed. Strive for perfection. Do not be easily swayed by the circumstances around about you. Look up! Look up! For your salvation truly does draw nigh. Even this day the sky is growing dark and My hand of judgment will not be stayed.

Joshua 24: 15 NKJV "And if it seems evil to you to serve the Lord, choose for yourselves this day whom you will serve, whether the gods which your fathers served that were on the other side of the River, or the gods of the Amorites, in whose land you dwell. But as for me and my house, we will serve the Lord."

~~~~~

Daughter now is the time for all things to come full circle around. I have been preparing My children for such a time as this. All that I have spoken in the past is now being brought full circle around. Take heed to My warnings children, for I truly am coming as the Great I Am. I am coming with the Sword of My Spirit and I am separating and dividing. I am separating the wheat from the chaff, and I am moving forward with My battle plans. There is so much being said that is not of Me, but there is also so much being said that is of Me. Discernment is needed in this end time revelation of My Spirit. My children need to be walking in total discernment at this given time. You must discern the signs of the times. Take no heed about tomorrow, for there is so much to do this day. Look to each day as a new adventure in Me.

Time is growing so short as you know it church. Now we are working in My Time! My Time goes very quickly and much is accomplished in a very short time. Feed not on the things of yesterday, but keep moving forward. Keep your eyes totally and completely on Me at all cost. For the cost is high. Many have paid the true price of repentance and they are going forth in My Might and in My Power and they are accomplishing many feats for Me and My Kingdom. But others have not gone down the road of repentance and they are not moving forward, but they have become stagnant and they are giving into the powers of darkness. But the light shall always prevail, no matter how dark the hour becomes. I have given a promise in My Word to My Remnant, and I shall keep that promise.

Do not be concerned about the signs wonders and miracles, but instead be concerned about the lost souls that need to be nurtured and brought into My Kingdom. I am supplying a way in the wilderness for all those who are truly seeking that way. I am giving them the very desires of their hearts and you will soon see many arise on the front lines that you thought were not going to make it.

Rejoice over these prodigals and help them come up higher. Cover them with My Blood and give them the **grace** I have given unto you. Many lives are still at stake. Many lives still standing in the valley of decision. Hold fast My church. Hold fast to the truths in My Word and never allow man to pull you astray with their cunning fables. My Word holds Power and it holds authority. My Word is powerful to pulling down the strongholds of darkness. Arise Church. Take your stand and follow Me at all cost. For as I said before, the cost is high.

~~~~~

How Holy are My People? That is a question each one of My Children should ask themselves, for I am coming after a Holy People; a church without spot or wrinkle.

Church, you are not ready to carry My Glory in all its fullness. I have earmarked a few that are Holy vessels to carry this Glory, but I need so many more.

There are strongholds in your lives that must be torn down. The enemy has placed a garrison around those strongholds and he is holding tight to My people. You have the weapons of Warfare to destroy any stronghold. Church, start destroying the strongholds!

Go before the throne of **grace** and receive Power to do the battle that lies before you. I am not short on Power. I will give Power to all that seek it.

Now is the time for total and complete freedom in My Body. This is the year of total Jubilee and Restoration in My Body.

I am your Friend. I am not your enemy. Take My Word and believe it and trust Me and then taste and see that I am good. I have spoken and so shall it be. As it was in the days of Noah so it is today. Get ready church. Do not be standing on the sidelines looking on and realizing that you have missed My Glory. For truly as I speak, some will miss this next mighty move of My Glory and there will be great gnashing of teeth, but they will realize it is too late.

Time is running out, quicker than you think.

~~~~~

THE GREAT I AM has come into your midst this night. I have come to fellowship with My Children. I am here to heal; to deliver; to set free. I am here to break every bondage. I am here to meet each and every desire. I am here to do a brand new thing within each and every one of you. I AM IS HERE!

I have brought healing in My wings this night. Healing for the broken hearted.

Healing for the spiritually dead. Whatever you need healed, I have brought it here this night. Reach out My children and touch the hem of My garment tonight.

Receive all that you have need of, for I am pouring myself out to you this night. I am pouring myself over this place. I am giving you everything that I am and everything that I will be.

Come My little ones, come to Me unashamed. Come to Me naked. Come to Me just as you are. Touch the hem of My garment, and allow Me to pour My healing virtues through you.

I love you with an everlasting love. I have never left you nor forsaken you even in the very throes of hell when you stood there in your deepest sin, I stood beside you; I wept over you; I held your hand. I set My **grace** and My mercy over you.

But I am here this night as the GREAT I AM, for I have seen each and everyone of your hearts I know the deepest intent within your hearts, and I am here to remove all the rubble within your hearts I am here to take away all that the enemy has placed upon you. I am here, touch Me this night. Touch Me this night and see if I will not remove the hay and the stubble. See if I will not take away all the pains of the past. And see if I will not take you forth into a brighter future than you have ever known or dreamt of.

THE GREAT I AM has spoken to you. And I AM says, I am here in your midst.

~~~~~

As you wait upon Me in the wee hours of the morning, I will share My heart of discomfort with you. My heart is heavy with the anticipation of what is coming upon My people in America and I am grieved because all of this could have been avoided, if only My people who are called by My name would have fasted and prayed as I commanded them to do, but to no avail. They were too busy with their own little meetings and to wrapped up in their own little worlds to give Me the time that I so desired to fellowship with them.

Truth is being shed abroad in this country and My truth shall be seen throughout the continent of America. Faith will arise within My people and they shall seek My face as never before. They shall see the rise and fall of a Mighty nation. They shall know what it is to sit in the comforts of their homes only to be uprooted and thrown into a state of frenzy as they try to escape My hand of wrath. The pleasures of this world will grow strangely dim and My people will run to the shelter of the Almighty once again and this time they shall stay under the shadow of the Almighty.

Who shall believe My report? Who shall stand upon the Holy Mountain and proclaim My judgments upon an unholy nation? My prophets will believe and My prophets will be sent forth to proclaim My word in Holiness and in My strength and in My power. Fire shall proceed out of their mouths and great signs and wonders will appear all around them. They shall see nation rise against nation and they shall see the Mighty fall, for this is My judgment upon this unholy nation.

Circumstances are about to change around about My Holy Ones! They shall come into the throne room of grace and receive My **Grace** in great abundance. They shall perceive My call upon their lives and they shall come running into My Holy Arms. For Holiness is where I am at. I am not in the facade of this world religion. I am in My Throne room of Holiness ministering salvation to My true prophets that have set at My feet and listened for My voice and have gone forth prepared and equipped to deliver salvation unto My people. Circumstances are about to change, as I have spoken many years ago. All those who have been warned and did not heed My warnings, will undergo a drastic change in their lives and they will stand amazed at the wonder of what I have done, and in the knowledge that they have missed the very best that I had for their lives. Listen intently to My voice little ones and do not stir from your place of worship until you hear My words of instruction; for this is a time of an unholy war that will ravage all those that did not have discernment of the times.

Harvest...

[29] But when the fruit is brought forth, immediately he putteth in the sickle, because the harvest is come.

HARVEST

~~~~~

Daughter, tell My people that I HAVE COME and I HAVE ALREADY started the perfect works in My churches all across this land. I am removing those who will NOT bow their knees to ME. I have given them more than enough time to change gods.

I am now about My business of GROWING UP My Church into the church that I have called her forth to be. She will shine in the gross darkness and she will bring the light to the lost and dying world; and she will go out into the streets and she shall proclaim the gospel to the lost and the dying. She shall bring in the harvest that is white unto **harvest** and she shall do great and mighty exploits in My name; for this is the hour and this is the time that I have spoken about in Joel chapter 2 and this is the church's divine appointment. She shall see Me in all My Glory and she shall understand heavenly principles as never before. She has only touched the hem of the garment until now and now she shall embrace the complete Godhead and she shall go forth empowered by the supernatural anointing of the Godhead.

I am restoring and I am tearing down. I am uplifting and I am casting down. Everything that exalts itself above me will be brought low. No more shall Baal reside in the temple of God. I am removing all the dross and all that will remain is My Glory. The church is becoming real once again and that real will attract the lost and the dying.

Come away My Beloved Church and fulfill your destiny in Me.

~~~~~

It will come from the North; it will come from the South; it will come from the East; it will come from the West. My holy fire mingled with My glory will sweep all across this land and it will consume a people that have made themselves ready for My use.

Where there was violence amongst (My people) there will be peace; for My people will begin to work together and they shall pull the walls of the adversary down and they shall reap a mighty **harvest** of souls through their unity.

The wind will blow and it will blow against My people and a freshness will be felt all across this land; for the wind will blow all that is not of Me off of My people; and when they go out it will be with the fresh new wind blowing forth from them and it will change the atmosphere and make it conducive for My Spirit to move mightily.

First you will see the great **harvest** of souls followed by mighty signs, wonders and miracles. Joel chapter 2 will be played out before your very eyes.

~~~~~

Father, please speak to your daughter:

Why should I speak any longer little one? There is no one that is paying attention to what I am saying. You have cried out and you have cried out, but to no avail. The peoples are dull of hearing and they have hardened their hearts to the wooing of My Spirit. Where do they think their help is going to come from? Where do they think they are going to hide when it all comes together? There is no place to hide from Me; absolutely no place.

I am a merciful, just god and I do not want any to perish; but I cannot help those who refuse My help. I will not allow them to hinder the move of My spirit that I am bringing across this nation. This nation is getting ready to be struck by the mightiest move of the Spirit that the church has ever seen and so many are going to be left out. There will be great weeping and gnashing of teeth on that great and marvelous day.

Did I not call my peoples to jump into the river? Did they jump into the river? No! Absolutely not! They stood on the river bank watching to see what I would do with this generation. Well, as I said in that day, it is now too late to get in the river. Did I not tell them not to stand in the river of compromise, but to jump into my river of living waters?

Daughter, the hour is so late and so much to be accomplished; but the body is not able to fight, so I have now turned to the highways and byways and I am compelling the lost and dying sinners to come into My presence and I will give them the fullness of My joy and they shall go forth gathering in this great **harvest** of lost souls.

Sing ye barren, those who have not borne children; for I am about to give you more children than you can number. As I told Abraham the stars are without number.

It is time to sit in the counsel, the full counsel of the most high and get every instruction straight from the throne of grace and do not allow man to deviate you from the path I have set your feet upon.

Isaiah 54: 1 NASB "Sing, o barren, you who have not borne! Break forth into singing, and cry aloud, you who have not travailed with child! For more are the children of the desolate than the children of the married woman," says the lord.

Genesis 15: 5 NKJV Then he brought him outside and said, "look now toward heaven, and count the stars if you are able to number them." and he said to him, "so shall your descendants be.'

Matthew 8: 12 NKJV "But the sons of the kingdom will be cast out into outer darkness. There will be weeping and gnashing of teeth."

~~~~~

Church open up your arms wide and receive all that I am about to send into your midst. I am about to unleash My glory in all its abundance and you shall see a great **harvest** of souls begin to come into My houses.

Only those that have love abounding will I use at this given hour. You must not look upon their appearance, but you must look beyond what you see on the outside and allow Me to show you the inside. I am more than enough. I am more than enough. Embrace Me and My love and allow Me to shine through you.

It is very vital at this given time that you embrace My agape love and then begin to allow it to pour through you to the lost and dying world.

~~~~~

This is not the time to be running to and fro looking for advice from others. This is the time to stay focused upon My face and to sit at My feet, knowing that I have all that you have need of and that I will supply all that you need to know and understand at this given time in your walk with Me. I am a faithful and a just God and I am taking care of My peoples that are called by My name.

Many false witnesses are running to and fro and speaking thus saith the Lord, and they have not been sent by Me, but they are on their own timetables and they have their own agendas. All will soon see and know that I am a true and loving Father that only wants what is best for His children.

Time is running out for My people. They must come into the inner circle of My arms and they must sit at My feet for instruction, or they will be swept away by the false and will never understand the true. Many false prophets have arisen upon the scene and they will shake the nations with what is not of Me, saith the Lord. Discernment is much needed at this given time and great wisdom is demanded of My peoples.

Job knew My voice, but there were times when he wondered just exactly what was going on around about him. Come under the protection of My holy mountain and you shall not be deceived nor will you be led astray with every wind and doctrine.

My people, truth must be sent forth and only My prophets can send the truth forth. My prophets, hear what I am saying at this given hour and understand the complete importance of what I am saying. I am requiring a time of fasting and prayer from each of My prophets at this given time. It is as you fast and pray, that you will hear the true voice of the Father and have discernment for this end time display of My hands at work in this unholy nation.

Rejoice before Me, and come bearing gifts of fasting and prayer and see what I will reveal unto your very hearts and eyes. For great visions will I give unto My peoples and great understanding of My Holy Word.

Spots. Do not allow any spots nor blemishes appear upon your most holy garments, but come before Me rejoicing, knowing that I am about to pour out the very core of My heart to My prophets and they will know all things pertaining to My end time word.

The glow of My Holy Wisdom will be evident upon My peoples and all will know that you have set at My feet as Moses did. Have I not been saying that you would see Me face to face? Have I not said that as I was for Moses, so I will be for you? I am becoming the Great I Am, to all those that will pay the price with fasting and prayer. Your heart will reveal yourself to you. Pay no attention to the voices of discord around about you, but stay focused upon My voice and My direction at this given time.

Holiness shall prevail in My chosen vessels at this given time. Knowing what is ahead will be apparent to all that hear My servant's voices. Seek not the wisdom of this world, but stayed focused on the wisdom from above. For it is from above that all wisdom will fall.

What is it that you are looking for? That is the question that I am sending forth for all to hear at this given hour. Is it a reed shaken by the wind? Or is it the truth that will come forth from My Holy Servants? **Matthew 11:7**. This is the day and this is the hour of Holy Redemption in the land and I am sending forth the **harvesters** at this given time. Many will find themselves on the road and many will find themselves with a change of authority and position. Be still and know that I am God and be still and hear the still small voice that will lead, guide and direct at this given time in My Kingdom. For I am giving Kingdom authority to My chosen vessels and they shall see truth restored to the House of the Lord. Truth shall prevail and many souls will be brought into the Kingdom, for this is the day of the **harvest** of lost and dying souls. The **harvest** truly is ripe unto salvation, and many have been waiting for this day and this hour. Seek not your own ways, but continue to seek My ways saith the Lord, for I am about to do a great and mighty works upon this land and all will soon see the I am in control of the heavens and the earth.

~~~~~

The first shall be last and the last shall be first, for I will not be mocked. I am tired little one, just as tired as you are and I am moving across this earth and many will die at this given time. There will be a mass slaughter of those who have set in My house and continued to indulge in their sins.

Yes, this is the year of Great Grace, but there are those who still refuse to give to Me those things that so easily beset them. They enjoy the lust of the flesh and they continue to go back to the fleshpots of this world. I am tired. So very tired. And I must take action. I have been crying repent for 2000 years now and still they serve Baal. What can I do, I ask you now, what can I do? I must avenge the blood of My Son, for it is crying out from the ground just as Abel's blood cried out for revenge. I must do what I have purposed in My heart to do, just as they continually do what they have purposed in their hearts to do. Shame upon shame has been brought upon Me. Blasphemy upon blasphemy. What a disgrace. What shame. It must be repaid. Does not My word say whatsoever you sow, that you shall also reap? Well, it is **harvest** time and I am the **harvester**. Stand back I say, stand back. For the bloodshed will be great, but the number of My church will grow through all this bloodshed. No more time to wait. I must act quickly.

~~~~~

As you sit in My presence, you will feel the warmth of My hand and you will feel the wind of My breath upon you. You will know that this is the season of great triumph for My body. As you flow in My spirit, you will experience the move of the supernatural and you will know that I am all around about you at every given moment. My touch is a special touch and a touch like no other. Those who have experienced this touch are never the same. I am touching My chosen ones in a new way. I am coming forth in all My glory and power at this given season and the world will never be the same.

Much is transpiring in this nation and much more is about to transpire. I am moving in unprecedented ways across this nation. Nation shall rise against nation, but My plan of salvation will not be stopped. All those who have believed in My name shall not be ashamed, for I will bring My glory to rest upon them and they shall know that I Am Lord of the **harvest** and I have truly come upon the scene in an unprecedented way. My ways are not your ways and believe me; all will soon learn this truth.

As nation rises against nation, My glory shall become stronger and stronger, for I am bringing My glory without measure and all things are becoming possible. The tower of Babel is nothing in comparison to what I am about to do across this nation. It has always been line upon line and it will always be line upon line. My chosen generation will finally rise up and take their rightful place among the nations and go forth with great signs wonders and miracles following them. No more little I's and no more big I's. Just one body with one mind doing the work of their Father in heaven.

Take notice of what I have already done around about you and then magnify that a thousand times and you will get just a small glimpse of what I am about to do.

Strike up the band, church and start marching, for I am on the move and this time I will not stop. Go forth in complete glory and know that I am with you all the way. This is My time and this is My season and the enemy has no say so. What I have spoken shall surely come to pass. The laborers are being sent forth into the **harvest** field and the great **harvest** is being reaped at this given season. No more, church, no more will the enemy stop the flood gates of heaven. I have spoken and so shall it be.

~~~~~

Daughter, the light has been sent out to the gentle dispensation (those who have not heard My Word) and you shall see a great influx of souls come into My houses at this given time.

Great crusades will be held all over this nation.

Stadium after stadium will be filled to capacity.

My power and My glory shall be seen in manifested ways in these meetings.

I have brought My sword and I have cut off the enemy's head at this given time.

No more sorrow, but total and complete rejoicing.

My houses that have been dens of thieves will now become My houses of prayer.

No more ungodly assignments from the shepherds, only My glory will be displayed.

Go back to the beginning church and take up your cross daily and follow Me. I am the alpha, omega, beginning and the end. I am in full control of this mighty move of My Spirit.

Many will rejoice at this move and many will stumble and fall. But My Glory will be revealed at last across this mighty nation.

Line upon line, precept upon precept. That is how it has always been and that is how it is right now.

Take courage, strong hearts! Take courage! For the maker has come just as He has promised, to sweep across this land with a mighty move of My Spirit.

Note about the coming **harvest**: When God refers to the gentiles. He is referring to the remainder of the gentile **harvest** or the gleanings. The gleanings (corners) of the field still are left. The main **harvest** is completed! The gleanings still have to be completed.

~~~~~

As My Word is, so am I. My word will never come back to Me void. What I have spoken shall come to pass. There are many out there who are seeking for things that are just not going to happen. I want My chosen generation to come forth knowing who My Son is and knowing what I will do for them, as they take up their sword and go forth in My might and in My power and glory.

Small seeds are now going to be big seeds. For I have taken the seeds that you have planted many years ago and I am producing a **harvest** of souls for this generation unlike any other generation. There will be no big I's or no little I's all will be equal in My eyes, for I have brought forth a most unique generation. No, you cannot see it at the present, but you shall.

I am above and not beneath. I am the head and not the tail. I am in complete control of all things and I am bringing forth the supernatural for all to see. Step into the waters church. Step into the waters, for they are running deep and they are running wide and all shall partake of the waters, if they thirst.

No more busy days doing nothing. The days ahead will be filled with much activity for the advancement of the Kingdom of God. I will in no wise turn any aside, for I am calling deep unto deep and there are many responding to this call at this very moment.

Salvation upon salvation is on the horizon. In the market place; in the schools; in businesses; in homes. You shall see salvations all around you. You will be totally amazed at who does come into My Kingdom and who stands on the river banks watching as the Mighty Rushing River carriers My true servants into the deepness of Me.

Stand back and be amazed church, but also go forward with My might, My power and My authority and accomplish all that I ask you to accomplish. This is the hour and this is the day of great salvations.

~~~~~

More than enough! I am the God of more than enough! I am supplying all of My children's needs according to My riches in Glory. Many seeds have been sown into good fertile ground and they are springing up at this given time and many will see the bountiful harvest of the seeds they have sown in the past. I have given My children promise after promise and I will bring each and every one of them to pass. Children, take no thought of tomorrow, for I am well able to keep you.

You have sown much into your harvest field and much is being brought forth at this given time. So many little seeds, but wait and see how big of a **harvest** all those little seeds bring forth.

You have thought your seeds meant nothing, but you will stand in complete awe as you reap a bountiful harvest at this given time.

Many, many housewives have sown into the Kingdom of righteousness, never expecting anything in return, but I always send back a return and now is the time of their **harvest**. All the tears that have been spent over the years are right now bringing forth a bountiful **harvest** of souls. Many lost loved ones are now going to come forth on bended knees and follow Me with all their hearts.

I am about to raise up a totally new generation of believers. They will not walk in doubt and unbelief like this stiff-necked generation, but they will take My word and run with it, no holds barred.

Just come expecting and see what I can do, saith the Father.

~~~~~

Tell My faithful followers that I truly am coming with healing in My wings. Healing of their land; healing of their finances; healing in their families; whatever needs healing, I am coming with healing in My wings.

I am the master healer and I am on the way with blessing after blessing. There is none other like Me and I fail not. Come My beloved ones, come unto Me all who are heavy laden and I will surely give you rest.

This is the time of **harvest**. The **harvest** is anything you have need of. It is a **harvest** of promises that are yet to be fulfilled. It is a **harvest** of plenty. Come and receive your **harvest**.

Some are asking, where am I? I am right here. I am right on time. I never arrive late and I never arrive early. I have a perfect timing for all things.

~~~~~

My church will know Me as LORD real soon, for they shall see My mighty hand move through My congregations and they shall see Mighty changes take place all across this nation. I have spoken so many things to My church, but only the remnant trusted and stood firm. Now My remnant will move forth in great strength and in the power of My Holy Spirit. My glory will follow them where ever they go. Just as the cloud lead My children in the wilderness, so My cloud will lead My chosen few today.

There will be much chaos all across this land, but in the midst of this chaos My mighty army of believers will emerge with the strength, power and fortitude that will be needed to lead My people to higher ground.

All the trials, tests, and tribulations that My body went through will now reap a mighty **harvest** of souls. It will be worth it all, saith the Father, for I have chosen such a time as this to show Myself strong on behalf of the faithful ones that stood the course and did not give into the wiles of the enemy.

Oh, such rejoicing will be heard in the camps all across this nation. It will not be in just one camp, but it will be in many all across this nation. I have been moving line upon line, precept upon precept and in perfect timing and My Time has now come. Not the people's time table, but My time table has now come, saith the Lord.

~~~~~

Tell My people to let go and allow Me to be God. I have great understanding of the times. Others are speculating. Know that I am in complete control of all things. This is the time of great **harvesting**. Go forth and bring the great **harvest** in. I am the Great I Am and I have given the orders to My holy angels to go forth and release this harvest of souls. Time is growing shorter every day. Time no longer exists as you once knew time. Time has been accelerated and there is not much time left. The clock is ticking away the minutes and each minute you waste only brings you closer to the end of this dispensation. Don't waste any more time, but cling to My promises and go forth into the greatest **harvest** in the history of the church.

Conquer the enemy on every side. Do not be intimidated by the enemy. He has lost all power and the saints can go forth and complete the race I have set before them in complete confidence that all is well with their souls.

~~~~~

Tell My children to let go of all that hinders and binds. Tell them that I want to be in total and complete control of all things in their lives and ministries. I am about to unleash My glory in an unprecedented way and there cannot be any hindrances to this movement. I am about to send forth the Elijahs to do a complete works for Me. There will be no limitations on My people. They will be able to accomplish all that I have set their hands to do. They will go forward with My strength and My ability to finish what I call them to start.

Know this day that I am calling all My chosen ones to step forth into the front lines and lead My people to freedom and victory. They shall know no boundaries. All they will know is complete joy in the Lord and they shall know what it is to conquer on all sides. Oh, I have chosen this day and this hour to show Myself strong and mighty to My church.

Glory will abound on all sides.

Come forth My bride and take your rightful place in My kingdom. I have hand picked all of you and you know that I have called you for such a time as this, so come forth and take your rightful place in My glory and bring in the vast harvest of souls that I have placed before you. It is time! It is time! It is time to go forth and conquer on all sides, for My glory has been released and My glory shall abound all over this continent.

There shall be no greater time than this for My church. This is the glorious time that I have been talking about and you shall see mighty movements in the days ahead. Mighty movements of My glory. For My glory shall abound on all sides and no one shall be able to stop this movement.

I have spoken and so shall it be.

~~~~~

If My people would only pray!

If My people would only trust and believe in Me!

If My people would only turn around and go in the direction that I have mapped out for them! If only!

What a difference there would be in their lives. They would have all that they desire. They would walk in the abundance of My blessings They would have more than enough so they could help the poor and needy. If only!

I say unto you My true church. Rise up out of the ash heap of despair and walk in the abundance of My promises. I have promised My true church everything.

There are so many souls out there just waiting to be **harvested** but My church will not respond to My voice They are so caught up in their everyday mundane affairs that they cannot hear My voice over the clanging of this world. Rise up church!

Rise up out of the ash heap of despair and allow Me to lead, guide and direct your footsteps.

Does not My word tell you that: The footsteps of a righteous man are ordered by the Lord?

Psalms 37:23

Well, I am trying to order your footsteps and you will not allow me to do so. Come away beloveds and forget the mundane things of this world and allow Me true entrance into your heart and lives and allow me to transfer My power and My glory into your mortal bodies.

This transfer will allow you to go forth in total strength to do My bidding. I am calling!

The hour is late!

Are you listening?

~~~~~

My little ones, this is a time of complete refreshing for My elect ones. You are going on a journey that shall take you to distant countries and faraway places. There is so much that you must accomplish for Me and My Kingdom and so very little time to do this.

Never before have you gone this way and it will be a glorious ride.

Know that I am in total and complete control of all things and I will do the impossible at this given time. The **harvest** is so ready and My workers are getting excited and now is the time for the complete release of My Glory Cloud.

~~~~~

Daughter there will be a devastating earthquake across the Midwest, but this will not be THE earthquake. Many, Many lives will be lost during this earthquake and much, much devastation. They would not believe Me when I said the shaking would occur. They would not believe Me when I said much destruction was coming across the land. They won't even believe this revival is of Me. Don't you see little one? Don' you see why I must do what I am doing? Like Nineveh, the peoples just would not get it right. Now I must destroy. Many, many nations will be affected by this destruction. Even today, they will not believe My prophets. Why do the nations rage? Why do the nations come against a Holy God? WHY! I will tell you why. They have sold themselves over to the strong delusion. They have stepped all over My Word and perverted it to suit their own vain imaginations. You shall see shortly a great earthquake of My Holiness. For I shall surely get My people's attention. I shall surely do a great and mighty works among the nations. For this is the final **harvest**. This is the final thrust for souls before the Great day judgment. Holy, holy, holy is the Lord God Almighty and so shall My peoples be Holy as I am Holy.

~~~~~

A summit meeting is occurring even as we speak little one. I have called upon My Holy Angels and the plans are being set into motion. This is not the beginning of the tribulation, but it is the beginning of sorrows. Man can say all that he wants to say, but I will have the last word in all matters. These are trying times for My whole nations.

Bitter will become sweet as the days go forth, for those who have chosen to follow Me.

I have given My true church a promise and I am well able to keep that promise. These trying times are producing strength in My Family of true believers. It is now that My true church will get extremely serious with Me and seek My face with much fasting and prayer. As this occurs, I will answer from heaven. I will give divine direction to all that call upon the name of Jesus.

How I long to sup with My true children. How I long to sup with the whole world, but sad to say, the whole world does not desire to sup with their maker.

Many, many souls will come into the Kingdom at this given time. I will place My true people at strategic places and the **harvest** will come in. I have been speaking about this day for quite some time now and now that day has come upon My church.

Why do they argue? Why do they not seek My face? They are so quick to judge My prophets. If only they would stop, turn around and face Me and only Me, all this division would stop. The enemy is already at work separating and dividing. Many sorrows are coming upon the nations. Oh if only they would be like My son David and turn from their wicked evil ways and repent.

Yes, I am a loving Father. But loving fathers correct their children, so they won't go astray. I am correcting all who will allow.

~~~~~

Daughter, it is going to shower down rain like you have never seen. It will be the former and the latter rain together, but the Latter Rain will be stronger and the latter rain will bring in the greatest **harvest** of church history.

This will be a historical event. It will be an event that will cover the entire globe. It will be of such magnitude that football stadiums will not be able to house the peoples. This move will far surpass all that the hearts have dreamed of. I am on the move and I am not stopping. Come on little one, come up higher and bring My people with Me. This is the event that all creation has been waiting on. This will usher in the second coming of My Son.

Everybody is talking about the Day of Pentecost in Acts, but this will stretch their minds. This outpouring will bring so much joy and peace to My peoples.

Daughter, tell them to dance! Tell them to leap for joy! Tell them to bust out the seams and get ready to build. For I have spoken and so shall it be.

I just see Jesus laughing and laughing and laughing. He is so victorious looking in the spirit realm. He is so pleased with what is about to happen. He is saying: Come on peoples come up higher and get in this boat with Me and see what I will do.

~~~~~

When it rains, it pours and I am beginning to rain upon My people and I am going to pour out the blessings that I have been promising them for quite some time now. You will see an abundance of **harvest** pouring in also. I am pouring out My Spirit upon all flesh at this given time and an abundance of Glory will be spread all across this land.

Roll over, roll over, roll over and receive all the blessings that I have for you at this given time. Truly it is blessing time all across this land for My Chosen Generation. I am pouring out My spirit in an unprecedented way. Come to the waters and drink of the fountain of living waters and allow Me to pour over you all the riches of My Kingdom.

Oh, My Church; My Mighty church rejoice in Me in this hour, for this is the hour of total blessing. I have decreed the thing and it shall come to pass. I am the Almighty One and I am blessing all who can stand to be blessed.

In the Spirit I could see our Father laughing and rejoicing over His people. Saints, just receive all that our Father has promised us at this given time.

~~~~~

Every year from this moment forth tribulations upon this earth will become more severe.

These tribulations are leading up to the great Armageddon and the rapture of My true church.

The winds of doctrines' have been sweeping across this land too long now and I am about to bring the entire truth of my gospel to this lost and devastated church era.

The time is ripe for the great harvest of souls and my church is still trying to get herself ready.

But I have no more time to wait. Those in my churches who are ready I am going to expose to this lost and dying generation and those who are not ready will miss out on this mighty move of My Glory.

I am ready and I am coming ready or not. Time has been exposed and things must begin to be **harvested;** for I will not lose one soul that I have predestined to be in my Glory.

~~~~~

To the remnant; the forerunner generation. I am asking you to stand still and watch the salvation of the Lord at work on your behalf. There is mighty warfare going on around about you, but have I not said that I will encompass you around about? Be strong warriors and go forth proclaiming the salvation of the Lord to all that you meet. This is salvation time and it is time to gather in the **harvest.** Come away from the cares of this world and run into the eye of the storm. I am sorry that you feel that I will not protect you, for that is far from the truth. Does not My Word say: No weapon formed against you shall prosper? Does it not say: Stand still and watch the salvation of the Lord at work on your behalf. I could go on and on, but you know My Word and what it says. Go forth now and conquer on all sides. Quit standing around waiting for the Glory to drop; for the Glory has already dropped and you do not have enough discernment to know it has dropped. Be sure in your heart that I am God and there is none other like unto me and then go forth dressed in your full armor and slay the giants of the land and take back what the enemy has stolen.

My beloved ones, I am not a man that I should lie and I say unto you this night, that I am more than able to conquer all of your enemies. Now you go forth and do the mighty works I have called you to do. Run into the eye of the storm when storms come and you will be safe there. Stay on the fringes of the storm and it will swallow you up.

Come now, it is time to lay aside all pretense and do the mighty works I have called you forth to do.

~~~~~

The grand scheme of things! You have no inclination of the grand scheme of things to come. I am preparing a far greater glory than anybody in church history can imagine. There will be so much going on, that it will astound the entire world. The church is about to make history once again. There will be a multitude of souls brought into the Kingdom at this given time; just like the days of Billy Graham.

Look out peoples for you will get burned by the fire if you are not securely wrapped in My presence. For the fires will burn brightly all over this land and many souls will be brought back from the dead (as it were). This has been a dispensation of death and I am coming to bring life and life more abundantly.

Forever changed! The peoples that jump into the river will be forever changed. I gave that promise a few years back and I am going to keep that promise. Many are looking unto me for their freedom and I will give them freedom from the bondages of sin and darkness. The gross darkness is creeping in all over the land; but my lights will burn brightly and they shall burn out all the chaff. Take heed little ones and do not let the little foxes spoil the vine.

Wherever you go all across this land you will see My glory; for once the glory comes in all its fullness, it will not cease. This is the times spoken of in Joel. Children, be sure you are steadfast in Me at this given time, for I am coming after a church that is without spot and wrinkle to help bring forth this great and mighty harvest.

Control! There will be no control; nor any manipulation. When My glory touches the peoples, they will be instantly changed. The money mongers will not have a chance to pull their little genie tricks and bilk the monies out of the peoples with false hope; for I will move so suddenly they will not have time to regroup.

The words I would say at this hour are: LOOK OUT! Look out for I am coming in all My Glory and all My Might and all My Power and nothing will be able to stop this mighty rushing river that will proceed out of the mouths of My Holy Ones.

Rejoice in the King of kings and the Lord of lords and do not be dismayed at anything you might see. Do not allow the profane things to come into the camp to spoil this move I am bringing upon the scene.

~~~~~

Consume: An all-consuming fire is going to come upon the church very soon little one and it will consume all of My people. Red, yellow, black or white even Muslim. It will surely cover all of My people. Lives will be instantly changed and rearranged. New songs will be sung and a new heaven will open up over my peoples. It will no longer be a heaven of brass, but it shall be an open heaven and they will have free access to everything I own.

What is it about this generation is your question to me continually?

Daughter, this generation is the closure of the church age. This generation will see the multitude of souls **harvested** for the Kingdom of God. This generation will usher in the signs, wonders and miracles. This generation has gotten so fed up with the church as usual, that they are going to become radicals for their Father and they shall go beyond what the church would even dare to imagine.

I couldn't get the present church to do this, so I had to raise up this generation of radicals.

Islamic Muslims will cover the earth, but they will not take over the earth. I am raising up a generation of believers that will have faith in My word and they will use the word to conquer on all sides. This generation of believers will be like none other. They will know the power and authority behind the name of Jesus and they will use that name and the Blood and the Water and they shall conquer nations on their knees. This is a radical bunch of believers and they shall shake the rafters with their praise and their worship.

Love…

Malachi 1:2 KJV

[2] I have loved you, saith the LORD. Yet ye say, Wherein hast thou loved us?

...

LOVE

~~~~~

I send you forth in this hour under the BANNER of MY LOVE to accomplish the task that I have set before your face. My BANNER of LOVE will melt the coldest of hearts and that BANNER of LOVE will bring My people full circle around.

Many strongholds will be broken at this given time through that BANNER of LOVE and many hearts that used to be cold and frigid will melt under that BANNER of LOVE that I am bringing forth.

There have been signs and wonders that did not melt the hearts or save souls.

It is My BANNER of LOVE that is going to do the complete works of the cross. After all;

Wasn't it LOVE that drove the cross to Calvary?

Wasn't it LOVE that placed the nails in My Son's Body?

Wasn't it LOVE that hung him there between heaven and earth?

LOVE started the works and LOVE will finish the work.

LOVE conquers all things, both big and small.

It is My LOVE that will compel them to come into the house of the Lord.

Trust Me, it will be by My LOVE that all men will know you.

~~~~~

Daughter of Zion write this upon the tablets of your heart and then rise up out of the pig sty and go forth and do the kingdom works. Write…

> Blessed are they who seek righteousness.
>
> Blessed are they that run into My arms in the midst of every storm
>
> Blessed are they that love the unlovable
>
> Blessed are they that feed the widows and the orphans
>
> Blessed are they that stand on My Word in the midst of the valley experiences
>
> Blessed are they who take My Word, use it as a sword and make the enemy bow his knees in every circumstance
>
> Blessed are the peacemakers for they shall inherit the Kingdom of God
>
> Blessed are you when they revile you for My names sake
>
> Blessed are you when you go down into the throes of hell and pull one soul out
>
> Blessed are you when you seek My face during every circumstance that life throws you

Blessed are you when the storms come to knock you off your feet, but you stand rooted and grounded in My Word

Blessed are you when above all you put on the armor of God and you plow fallow ground to plant fertile seeds into

Blessed are you!

You are blessed! You are blessed going in and going out. You are blessed in your storehouses and in your fields! You are blessed saith the Father.

I am your comforter. I am the great I am and I fail not My holy remnant that has chosen Me over the mundane things of this world.

Blessed! Blessed! Blessed!

~~~~~

Holy, Holy, Holy. Holy is the Lord God Almighty and Holy shall be My Children whom I have called out of darkness into eternal light. Come My Brethren, come into the light that I Have shed abroad for each of you to enter into. Be showered upon by My Shekinah Glory. Be endued with Power from on high. Be not conformed to this world, but be enlightened by My Word and then follow Me with all of your hearts and bring all that troubles you to the altar of incense and allow Me to consume all that burdens you down so you can go forward in My Might, Power and Strength and do the mighty exploits that I have called you forth to do. I am the way, the truth and the light and there is none other like Me in all this earth. Follow Me, little ones! Follow Me right on up into My Glory Cloud and allow Me to saturate you with My Glory and then send you forth into the nations to retrieve the people out of the snare of the fowler. I AM THAT I AM HAS

COME UPON THE SCENE and things will no longer be the same. I am changing and rearranging things even as we speak and you shall be totally amazed with the outcome.

LOVE IS THE ONLY WAY! Walk in My agape love and free the souls from the bondage of the evil one. It is your turn church. ARISE! SHINE! FOR YOUR GLORY HAS COME!

BACK/RETURN TO YOUR FIRST LOVE

~~~~~

Now you will see the great whirlwind of My Wrath run across this Nation. Now you shall see the mighty turbulence that I have been talking about. Turn My Children! Turn unto Me, the Father of your soul. I love you with an everlasting love and I am calling one more time for you to turn before it is too late. There is none other like unto Me. You wanted Baal--well I allowed you to have Baal for a season so you could see what he would give you. You have seen the destruction in your lives. You have seen that the enemy gives nothing good. You have lost much in this period of rebellion. Will you still play around with the things of this world or will you relent and **come back to your first love?** This decision belongs to you and only you. You are the decider of what goes on in your life, none other

~~~~~

Church! Wake up and see what is happening all around about you. My glory is going to cover all this gross darkness and many souls will be running into the houses of refuge that I have already set in place. Question to you! Are you ready to minister to all these frightened, lost souls? Are you dead to your own sins? Are you sold out to the cross? Church, you must ask yourself this question and be honest with yourself; for I am coming back for a spotless church, one without spot or wrinkle.

Have you learned to abide under the shadow of the Almighty or are you still running to and fro doing your own thing, thinking I am approving of your own thing?

Church you must **come back to your first love**. You must come worshiping and praising me with all your being. Come church— come and abide under the Shadow of the Almighty and allow Me to perform the miracles you need in your lives.

Am I not the same God today as I was in the beginning? Do I not do the same miracles as I did in the beginning? Then what is the problem? What are you looking for? Where are you going? Come church and abide with Me and allow Me full recourse in your life. For this is the hour of total and complete redemption for all My peoples.

Blessed are those who seek My face early each morning.

~~~~~

There is a new chapter being written in heavenly places for the church of tomorrow. Church has already changed and it will continue to change until it is where I want it to be. Church will no longer be man-made, but it will be driven by My Spirit. My Holy Spirit will be at the helm and man will not be in control, for we have entered into a new realm of Glory and in that realm all things will be manifested through My Spirit.

Worship will change drastically. You will see warfare music mixed with total worship. The warfare music will tear down the kingdom of darkness and the total worship will bring in My glory. Many souls will be set free and many souls will be raptured up into My heavenly places where visions will be seen of the great things coming to this earth.

I am not finished with My church. I have just begun! Man thinks I am leaving My Body of Believers, but not so. I have chastened and I have set apart and now I am ready to move with My glory cloud. Just as I led the children in the desert with My glory cloud, I am ready to lead My Church into her fullness of My glory.

Many that had fallen away because of woundedness will now return back to their first love and the enemies of their souls will be conquered. There will be no more running to and fro. For My Spirit shall prevail everywhere and My glory shall be seen upon My peoples.

It is harvest time. A great harvest of souls is coming into My Body. Great rejoicing in the throes of heaven and great moaning in the throes of hell, for the enemy's camp is being torn apart and the enemy has lost much ground because My people have learned to fast and pray. They have and are still learning to grab hold of the horns of the Altar and hang on and allow Me to guide them through the dark nights of their souls.

Oh, much victory in the camps all across the land. Much! Much harvesting of souls! A harvest like has not been seen in the annuals of history. But it is surely harvest time and the souls are crying out for relief from the pressures of hell.

Nation shall rise against nation. Wars and rumors of wars. But the ultimate destruction is not going to happen. I am preparing a mighty army of prayer warriors that are rising up and interceding for this nation and you shall see My Mighty hand at work all across this nation.

Time as it is known will not be in the days ahead. For time is moving into a different time zone and I must accomplish much for My Kingdom. Many saints will come on home to be with Me in this time frame. Much will be accomplishment for the gospel in this time frame.

My Word says "Not by might, not by power, but by My Spirit saith the Lord" and you shall see this come into fruition in this time frame. I am raising up a mighty army of warriors that are going to storm the front lines and take back the ground that was lost in the last generation of saints. You will see prayer return back to the schools. You will see Rowe versus Wade overturned. You will see men and women of God repent and return **back to their first love**. You will see the enemy defeated at every turn. This nation will be turned upset down for My Kingdom.

Many young ones will come into the call in this time frame. You will see revival break out in the schools all across this nation. You will see the colleges break forth into revival. You shall see the government overturned and a new awakening for truth come forth.

I am on the move and I am not going to stop. This is a time of great acceleration in the heavenly realm. The rain that is coming is going to drown My children in the river of My Glory. You will see those come in that you thought weren't interested in Me. You will see a mighty onslaught of the enemy, but it will not stop My church

BELIEVE THE FATHER...

~~~~~

Tell My Body to repent so that I can restore all that the palmer and canker worm have stolen. Tell them to repent for their disobedience and their stiff necks and their rebellious ways. I am a God of plenty and I CAN supply every need. I can undo the works of the enemy. I can conquer the enemies of their souls. But they must turn and repent and give me the leave way to do the things that need done in their lives.

How awesome am I? Ask yourselves that and then act on your answer. If you think I can do all things, than I will do all things. If you think I can do only some things, then I will do only some things. What can you believe for? What kind of God do you serve?

Why do you walk around looking down trodden when I have My storehouses full? Why?

Has not my word declared that I own the cattle on a thousand hills? Has not My Word declared that I can do all things according to My riches in Glory? Has not My Word said test me and see if I will not open the windows of heaven and pour you out a blessing that you cannot contain?

Do you believe My Word or is it just a fairy tale to you? Many are acting like it is just a fairy tale. Believe Me, it is not a fairy tale written by men. It is My solemn promises written and inspired by the Holy Spirit of truth.

Come now and let us reason together saith the Lord. Come and let us dine at the table I have spread for My Church. This table is full of all things and I desire to heap all these things onto your bosom.

You have not because you ask not and when you do ask you ask amiss. Shame upon shame. My Body brings shame to My Word daily. When, oh when Church are you going to repent of your wicked evil thoughts and ways and turn to me and allow Me to bless you as I desire to bless? WHEN?

I have spoken of My Glory Cloud, but how many truly believe My Prophets? Don't lie! You have spoken babbling words against My prophets that have spoken that My Glory is coming across the land. Stop! Turn Around and Repent before it is too late church. I have spoken about the great destruction coming across the land. I have spoken about the great falling away. It is all happening right before your very eyes, but yet you will not believe. I am not going to shake rattle and roll for you church. You must repent and turn. Then I will answer from My heavenly throne and then I will pour you out a blessing you cannot contain.

I have spoken much and I have spoken often, but if you have noticed, I have not spoken much lately. Can you blame me? You will not believe anything I say or do, unless there is a sign and a wonder attached to it. Well, get ready, for it is by faith and not by sight that I am coming to unfold My promises in My Word. You can take this to the bank. I am coming with Sword in one hand and a Banner of Love in the other. Which will you receive? Only you know the answer. But there is still a window of repentance open. Repent while there is still time, for the window is about to close on this dispensation and I am getting ready to harvest the world.

> **Isaiah 1:18-20 NKJV** "Come now, and let us reason together," says the Lord, "Though your sins are like scarlet, they shall be as white as snow; though they are red like crimson, they shall be as wool. [19]If you are willing and obedient, you shall eat the good of the land; [20]but if you refuse and rebel, you shall be devoured by the sword"; for the mouth of the Lord has spoken.

> **James 4:3 NKJV** "You ask and do not receive, because you ask amiss, that you may spend it on your pleasures.

CARRY MY LOVE, FORWARDING ALL MY LOVE

~~~~~

All those who are fed up with sin;

All those who have decided that they are ready to go all the way with their god;

It is you who I am getting ready to exalt;

It is you who I am getting ready to use in a mighty way;

It is you who will go all the way with the maker and the master of the universe.

You will **carry my love** to a love starved generation of lost and dying souls.

It is you that will have compassion and grace for the down and outers.

It is you who will carry the glory for all the world to see at this given time.

I am **forwarding all my love** to you and that love will saturate you totally and completely and it will be through this great saturation of love that many lives will be changed in a split second.

I have called and I have chosen a peculiar people for this end time revelation of who I truly am.

DISPENSATION OF MY LOVE...

~~~~~

Daughter, there is a new **dispensation of My love** coming across this land. The fatherless; the rejected; the bound will know of this great love and they will succumb to this love and I will use them to father many nations. The church has gone astray and will not humble themselves and turn and repent; therefore, I must go to the lost and dying and compel them to come into the house of the Lord (with this new love) and I will use them mightily to pull down the strongholds of darkness that prevail all across this great nation that I call America.

Idols will be torn down. New standards of holiness will arise upon the horizon and these peoples that once walked in total darkness will walk in the newness of life and they shall bring the light into a dark, dark world.

Church, where you have failed these new converts will prevail. They shall bring multitudes to the crossroads of life and they shall compel them to come into the house of the Lord.

You must muster up all the faith you have and you must increase your faith and then walk in the newness of life that I have laid at your feet and come and follow the Most High God and never look back.

This is total transition time; transition from the old to the new, old things being totally forsaken and walking in the newness of life that I have set before you.

This is the time to march church. March to the drum beat of the Most High God; put aside all your idols, and come follow Me, your personal savior.

EVERLASTING LOVE...

~~~~~

THE GREAT I AM has come into your midst this night. I have come to fellowship with My Children. I am here to heal; to deliver; to set free. I am here to break every bondage. I am here to meet each and every desire. I am here to do a brand new thing within each and every one of you. I AM IS HERE!

I have brought healing in My wings this night. Healing for the broken hearted.

Healing for the spiritually dead. Whatever you need healed, I have brought it here this night. Reach out My children and touch the hem of My garment tonight.

Receive all that you have need of, for I am pouring myself out to you this night. I am pouring myself over this place. I am giving you everything that I am and everything that I will be.

Come My little ones, come to Me unashamed. Come to Me naked. Come to Me just as you are. Touch the hem of My garment, and allow Me to pour My healing virtues through you.

I love you with **an everlasting love**. I have never left you nor forsaken you even in the very throes of hell when you stood there in your deepest sin, I stood beside you; I wept over you; I held your hand. I set My grace and My mercy over you.

But I am here this night as the GREAT I AM, for I have seen each and every one of your hearts I know the deepest intent within your hearts, and I am here to remove all the rubble within your hearts I am here to take away all that the enemy has placed upon you. I am here, touch Me this night. Touch Me this night and see if I will not remove the hay and the stubble. See if I will not take away all the pains of the past. And see if I will not take you forth into a brighter future than you have ever known or dreamt of.

THE GREAT I AM has spoken to you. And I AM says, I am here in your midst.

~~~~~

I have come into this place with My dominion and authority to set My captives free. Yes many curse words have been sent out. Yes many assignments are upon My children. Not just one, but many. But I am here this night in all My Glory. My presence abides within this place this night and I am breaking off every curse that has been placed

92

upon you. And I see your heart even this night. I have seen your thoughts. And I know that you are sorry for what you have said about others. I have received that sorrow. I have received it and I have set you free from it. I am cleansing your mouth this night from all curse words. I am cleansing your minds of all curse thoughts. I am setting your minds free.

I am placing you in the hollow of My hand. And the enemy will not be able to destroy you as he thought he would. He had purposed within his heart to take each one of you out. But this night I have determined that his curse over you is broken. And I have come. I have come to set the captives free. <u>And free you are</u>. It does not matter what you feel. It does not matter what your mind is still saying to you. You are free! Walk in that freedom. Walk in that liberty. Allow Me to have space to do the cleansing that needs to be done. Do not condemn yourself to hell. Do not torment yourself one day longer. Just give Me the space I need to cleanse you from all filthiness and all unrighteousness.

For the enemy has sent many, many assignments against each one of you. It has been like a plague throughout My Body and I am cleansing all of those who will allow Me to touch them. And even this night each one of you, in this place has allowed Me room and allowed Me space to come in and to do a deep cleansing. For this I want to tell you that I love you with **an everlasting love**. For this I say you have found favor in My sight. And for this I am going to restore all that the canker and palmer worm has stolen. For I see the torment in your heart. I see the torment in your soul. And I also know that the enemy's assignment over you is broken. And I have come and set the captives free, even this night.

You will see the day come when you will rest in calm assurance that I am yours and that you are mine you will see the day come that you have been seeking for, for so long. That you know, that you know,

93

that you know, that I have forgiven you, and that I have truly set you apart for My Kingdom. Embrace Me this night. Embrace the truth that I have spoken and know that I am in your midst and I will not depart, saith your Father.

~~~~~

Tell My children that I am with them wither so ever they go. Tell My children that **I love them** with an **everlasting love**. Tell them to prepare their selves for a mighty move of My spirit. I am coming on the waves of love and I am going to restore and refresh My Body. The battle has been long and bloody, but My true soldiers have endured the good fight of faith and have come forth victoriously.

A great landslide of souls is coming into the Body of Christ. Many salvations are riding on the wings of My Spirit. The church will grow from this moment forth and you shall see great rejoicing in My Body of Believers.

They are learning how to praise Me through all their troubles. They are learning to praise Me when they don't feel like praising. They are finally learning what it means to truly praise the living Father.

FATHER THAT LOVES/FATHER WHO LOVES...

~~~~~

Nation shall rise against nation, but My Glory shall rise higher. My Glory shall cover this entire earth. All will see Me for who I truly am. They shall know Me as God of this universe. They shall know that they have a triune **Father that loves** His children and will not allow them to go under. I know who are mine and I take care of My own. I never leave My children hanging. I am always with them. I am always leading, guiding and directing their very footsteps. They always know in what direction to go. They never flounder. I have a remnant that will come forth and they will wear My Glory and they will do great and mighty exploits for Me.

~~~~~

Daughter, write this down upon the tablets of your heart and remember this always, for this is from everlasting to everlasting. I am the triune **Father who loves** His children desperately. I will go to any lengths to provide for My chosen ones, those who continually call upon My name. I am not a harsh, bitter Father who desires to punish his children. On the contrary, I am just the opposite. I want to lavish all the perfect gifts upon My chosen generation. I do not want to overlook even one of My chosen generation. So many are being deceived at this given time. So many are being railroaded into thinking they should not have things, I desire to give all good gifts to My children. What did the father of the prodigal do? He lavished the very best on his son, when he returned. I want to do the very same thing to My chosen ones in this season of total and complete restoration.

Where have all the blessings of Abraham, Isaac and Jacob gone to? They are still in My heavens. I am just waiting to pour out a blessing that My children cannot contain. The enemy is trying to steal these blessings from My Body. Rise up out of your stupor church and do not allow the enemy to rob you of the blessings I have already begun to pour out upon My true church. My word does not lie (the wealth of the wicked truly is laid up for the righteous) Laugh in the enemy's face and look up and ask and then receive. Do not be ashamed of what you already have. Ask and you shall receive. Faith is the all-consuming blessing for My people. Those who have faith, ask and believe, they shall surely receive.

Oh how sad, that the enemy has been able to give my church another black eye over his lies. I tell you this, I will uncover the lies of the enemy and my church shall surely come forth bearing great gifts. What did I give My chosen ones when they left Egypt? It was not the scrapings, it was the very best. Come on church, look up, believe My Word, do not believe the lies of the antichrist. For right now, he has surely come to steal, kill and destroy. Do not allow the devourer to devour any longer. But look up and receive all the blessing I have for you.

THE STOREHOUSE IS COMPLETELY FULL!

FEEL MY LOVE/BE FILLED WITH MY LOVE...

~~~~~

Look up to the hills from whence cometh your help, little one. I am not a God that I should lie. What I have spoken shall surely come to pass. I am the Great I Am and I fail you not. Little one, the end is very near. Nearer than anybody thinks. But I have a multitude of worshipers that need to come to the full knowledge of who I truly am. I am the Great I am and there is none other like unto Me. Hold fast to what you have and allow Me to add to what you have. Do not be discouraged nor dismayed in the coming days. For I am moving amongst My people once again and this movement is geared at full restoration of all things that the palmer and canker worms have stolen.

Again I say hold fast and do not let go. The worst is over and the new is before your face. This new is full of Joy, Peace and great salvations. I am on the move. I am doing exactly what I have promised My Body that I would do. Now just hold on to what you have and do not compromise. Do not look back and do not get discouraged, for the best is yet to come.

Multitudes upon multitudes need to hear of My Son. I am sending the messengers with the good news, even as we speak. You will see the mighty climax of all that I am doing. You shall live and not die saith the Father. For I have a perfect works to do through My church at this given hour.

What you have sown church; you will now begin to reap. What you have sown in tears you shall reap in great joy. Come on church, it is time to dance. It is time to sing, for the victory is secure and the victory is already here.

Think not in your heart (this cannot be) for I have spoken it and so shall it be. Be tenderhearted to those who do not know Me and allow them the space to **feel My Love** and My Joy unspeakable. Allow them the comfort of falling in Love with their maker, the Great I Am.

Be slow to anger church and be **filled with My love** and go forth and conquer the nations for Me. And always remember that I am with you always, even unto the end.

GOD OF LOVE...

~~~~~~

The Gulf Oil spill is of me saith the Lord. They can scrutinize; categorize; blame, but when it comes to the end, they will know that it is I the Lord thy God that has caused this thing to happen. I build and I destroy. I bring peace and I bring disaster. Am I getting the people's attention? You had better believe I am. Some in the church circle know that this is my making, but they are unable to bring themselves to say so, for fear of rebuttal. But none the less, it is I.

I will allow them to cap it, but not before My complete works has been accomplished from the spill. You think I am fooling around when I say food will be scarce? You think I am chiding when I say the economy will collapse? You think I lie when I say that I will bring down the mega churches that are built on man? Wait and see people—

wait and see what a **God of Love** will do. I am doing this because I love my people you know. I love them too much to sit idly by and watch them slide into the throes of hell.

Tell my people to take heed to what they are hearing and what they are saying and tell them I cannot bless those who walk in fear of man.

Jonathan was a man after my heart, for he did not fear his father—he continued to love David no matter what the consequences. But what are my peoples doing? They are trying to overthrow my Word. They are trying to make My Son's Blood a mockery. Wait and see—just you wait and see who has the last word.

There will be trying times all across this land. The land will tremble under My Mighty Hand.

~~~~~

Tell My People THAT I AM COMING after a spotless bride, one without spot or wrinkle. Strife, envy, jealousy and vain imaginations can no longer fellowship with My Holy Spirit. My word says that I will not always strive with man. What does My Body think? I am a Holy God and I am a Just God and I am a **God of Love** and I am a God of Wrath. I have been displaying all of my virtues to My Body in hopes they would get it together once and for all. But to no avail. Listen up Church. I am coming, ready or not, I am coming.

~~~~~

I have spoken and so shall it be. My company of angels has been sent forth to do a mighty works in My churches all across this American continent. They shall not return until their works are complete.

Nation shall rise against nation. False prophets will continue to come upon the scene.

My church shall continue to be deceived by the mockers and scorners. For they have not abided under the Shadow of the Almighty. They have not heeded My voice in the critical hours of the night. They have followed in the footsteps of their idols and they not the hour of their visitation. Woe unto those who would prophesy peace unto this fallen nation. I am a God of Love first, but now I come as a Father full of wrath for a nation that has totally defiled My land and My Word. Woe and again I say Woe unto those inhabitants who have sought after their own pleasures and have left Me out of the picture. Woe, Woe, Woe. For the cup if indignation is full and I am pouring out My wrath upon this nation like never before.

Love! Who says I don't love my nation? **I love** this nation more than any other. But this nation has turned their backs upon Me and now I must repay.

~~~~~

Tell My people to flee My wrath to come. Tell them that I am coming on the scene with great wrath. I have asked, begged, pleaded for My children to come up higher, but they are refusing. Many leaders are leading My children astray. Many are saying I am not a God of wrath. I tell you My children, I am a **God of Love**, long suffering and patience first. Then I am a God of wrath. I have been loving; I have been long suffering; and I have been a God that is full of patience, but nothing has worked, so now I must bring My wrath upon a disobedient, stiff necked generation of Baal seekers.

HE LOVES…

~~~~~

There is a new moon on the horizon and with the new moon comes a full impact of My Glory. Not everyone will partake of this Glory, because they have not submitted themselves totally and completely unto Me, the one true creator. Many have already chosen the way of Baal. They are counter-productive in their works for Me. I have no more space for those that decided to dwell outside the inner court. I have heard the speculations of these people. They have decided that My prophets are false and they do not need to heed to their words. They do not want to comprehend that a Father would chastise those that **He loves**. But, I have spoken and so shall it be. Line upon line, precept upon precept. There is no other way. You must come to Me through My Son; you can come no other way.

My Word does not change.

I do not change.

I have spoken and so shall it be. There just is no other way.

I am the Truth and the Light and all must come to Me now, if they intend to partake of the heavenly throne room in paradise.

John 14:6-7 NKJV Jesus said to him, "I am the way, the truth, and the life. No one comes to the Father except through Me. "If you had known Me, you would have known My Father also; and from now on you know Him and have seen Him."

Luke 23:42-43 NKJV Then he said to Jesus, "Lord, remember me when You come into Your kingdom." And Jesus said to him, "Assuredly, I say to you, today you will be with Me in Paradise."

COUNTER-PRODUCTIVE having results contrary to those intended

I AM LOVE

~~~~~

The Body of Christ is not ready for what is about to hit all across America. The devastation will be so great; that it will take everybody by surprise. I have been speaking about this time, but few are listening. They have closed their ears to My Words and have opened themselves up for deception.

I am going to come in all of My Might and My Power and I am going to do a works that will astound all. This is the time of the great harvest spoken of in Joel and the harvest truly is white unto harvest, but where are those that are ready for the harvest?

Tell them I am coming and I am not holding anything back. I have pulled the plug (so to speak) and things and events will occur so swiftly that heads will reel.

My sovereignty will be seen by all. All will know that I am God. Those in the household of faith that would not relent will weep and wail for they will know that they have missed their day of visitation and they will know what awaits them on judgment day.

I am LOVE and I send forth LOVE; but the time has come to fulfill My Word; and fulfill My Word I shall. Stayed tuned for My Voice Church for I will begin to speak volumes to those who are listening and in those volumes will be instructions for this end time hour.

I STILL LOVE THEM…

~~~~~

101

Tell My people that this great onslaught of storms that is coming upon the economy cannot be avoided. They can be lessened, but they cannot be avoided. I gave many various warnings that these days of tribulation was coming upon this land, but not many heeded my warnings. But even now, I am willing to contend with My Peoples who are called by My name and I will bring them through this time of great tribulation. Many will run to and fro, but there will no place to find rest, except in Me. They must abide under the shadow of the Almighty, even now, while there is still time. For time is of great essence at this given time. Many who are called by My name will try to jump ship, but I am encouraging all to stay on board and do not allow the hollowness of man's words bring them down. I am encouraging My People who are called by My name to continue on their walk of faith with Me and turn from their wicked ways and follow Me with all of their hearts.

These have been times of great testing and trials and they are not over yet. A great catastrophe is about to occur that will send shock waves all over the world. Then My people will look up, but not until then. I am a Holy God and I require complete obedience from My Chosen People.

It is time for the rain to begin to fall upon the parched and drying land. It is time for My Glory to cover the whole earth. It is time and it is coming. Those who have and are still mocking Me, will know the truth and they will not be able to turn back. **I still love them**, but it will be too late.

Many would not commit themselves unto Me, the true and living God. But, I still have a remnant that has not bowed their knees to the world and its evil system.

I WANT TO LOVE ON THEM...

~~~~~

Daughter, take pen in hand and write. For many years now, the Body has been on their own course of destruction. I have been trying to get their attention, but to no avail. Now, I will get their attention. **I want to love on them**. I want to restore all that the palmer and canker worm have stolen. I want them to live in the blessings of Abraham, Isaac and Jacob even though the whirlwind is raging around about them.

I want to take them into the eye of the storm where they will be safe from the flying shrapnel. The debris will get thick and sometimes seem to overwhelm all of society but I want to wrap my precious ones in my arms of protection and shield them from all harm. I want my chosen ones to do a 100 degree turn and follow after me with all of their hearts. This is what I want. Will My precious ones heed and follow my desires or will they go on their own course of destruction?

Nobody! Absolutely nobody knows the day nor the hour of the return of My Son to bring My true Bride on home. Many are contemplating, but nobody knows the day nor the hour. I don't want their eyes fixed on His return. I want their eyes fixed on the harvest that is ripe. I am looking for the harvesters that will bring in this end time harvest. I am looking for those who are faithful to the words I speak into their ears in the wee hours of the morning. I am looking for the truly faithful ones in this hour. Those that I can trust with a lost, dying and hurting world! A world full of conflict and despair! A world spinning out of control!

Who are those that will say: Here I am Lord, use me?

LOVE ME/LOVE MY...

~~~~~

Many sorrows will begin to befall those who are refusing to follow Me. I have not asked much from My people, I have only asked that they **love Me** and follow Me, but there is so much chaos out there, to distract and sideswipe My people. They no longer look to the make as their supplier, they look to man they look to flesh. I desire to take care of My chosen ones, but they are so busy with the cares of this world that they leave Me out of the loop every day. I have asked My children to come close, but they worship Me afar. I am asking My chosen ones at this hour to be still and know that I am God and know that I am in full control of all things, in the spirit realm and in the natural.

~~~~~

Daughter, there is a mighty move afoot. I am staging the biggest finale that the church has ever seen. I am choosing the players for this play right now. I am choosing those who are committed to Me with all of their being. I will not choose a player that is halfhearted. I know those that are Mine and I am giving them their parts to play even as we speak. This is the finale of all finales. Who will partake of this great play? It will surpass anything Hollywood has put on. The world has seen nothing yet. Just you wait and see what I am about to do with and through My true church.

I am saying come away My beloved ones and partake of this great and final play that is already coming together in the heavenlies. Do not think this a light thing that I am doing at this given time.

I have been so gracious to those who **love Me** and My grace shall abound even more widely as the days progress. The show to stop all shows is about to begin. Who will play the major roles?

~~~~~

Why do My children always forsake Me? I am not asking you that question, I am telling you something. My children always forsake Me because they never knew Me in My fullness. They hear of Me. They want to hear My voice. But they never pay the ultimate price. SURRENDER.

They will not surrender their wills to Me. They play their silly games of hide and seek. They are always playing the harlot or the fool. They are the biggest compromisers that you will ever see.

Am I disgusted with this? Absolutely! That is why I am coming with the sword and many that call Me by name will fall by the sword. Remember Lot. He was told to take his family out of Sodom and Gomorrah, but it was a hard thing for him to do. His wife did not make it, because she was more attached to the world than to Me. Lot was caught up in the ways of the world also, but he chose Me over the world. But the vast majority of the church has chosen the world over Me. I wept for a season. I sent out My prophets to convince My church to turn. I sent My son's blood, but nothing would change their hearts. Now, the sword is coming and it cannot be stopped.

Much weeping and wailing will occur, but it will be too late. Unstop your ears church. Listen to what the Spirit is saying to My church. Fear Me. **Love Me**. Worship Me because the hour has turned late and for some there is no turning back, for their hour of repentance has passed them by.

Did I not warn, do not miss your day of visitation? Well, many did not heed that warning and their day of visitation is gone, never to come back. Woe; Woe; Woe unto those who went with their vain imaginations. They have over stepped the boundary line, never to return.

Daughter, I am getting ready to mobilize one of the biggest events in church history.

The armor bearers are in place and I have all heaven at attention.

Be sure you are in a secure place in Me when this event occurs. Once the event occurs, there will be no time to get in that secure place. I have been mobilizing this event for quite some time now and the time is now nigh at hand. There won't be any time to think. It will be sudden and everything will become the suddenlies. The line has been drawn in the sand and I am definitely on the move in the heavenly realm and I am bringing it to the earthly realm. You have been wondering what I am saving you for and this is it little one. The greatest adventure in history! The greatest triumph in history! Man has not seen anything like it, nor will it ever be seen again. This is going to be a once in church history event, never to be duplicated.

Arise and Shine, for your light has come.

Isaiah 60: 1 – 3 NKJV [1.] Arise, shine; For your light has come! and the glory of the Lord is risen upon you. [2.] For behold, the darkness shall cover the earth, and deep darkness the people; but the Lord will arise over you, and His glory will be seen upon you.[3.] The Gentiles shall come to your light, and kings to the brightness of your rising.

~~~~~

The atmosphere is becoming cloudier and cloudier. There is much deception going on in this United States. The government is so corrupt and the politicians are covering up so much debris. But watch what I am going to do. Watch and see what is going to transpire over the next two months of 2009. I am bringing My People to a total resting place in Me and they shall know Me as a triune God. They shall know Me as their Everlasting Father. They shall see Me face to face once again. Once again they shall stand on the precipice of Joy unspeakable and full of Glory. They will not be concerned about the persecution that rages around about them, for they shall be totally full of My Glory continually and they will have died out to flesh and they will stand for the sure words of My Word.

Daughter, there is going to be such a glorious time upon this earth. Great signs wonders and miracles will be manifested by those who truly **love Me** with all of their hearts. They will know what it is that they are working for at last and they will do it with gladness of heart. The enemy will be uprooted at every turn. True happiness once again shall prevail. My people will become another Paul; Peter; Isaiah and Moses. You shall see little one, you shall surely see Me manifest Myself amongst My peoples that are called by my name.

Rejoice; rejoice; for Rejoicing time is in the house. Sing praises unto Me, the King of Glory. Sing praises unto Me out of a heart of Joy unspeakable and full of glory. Sing; sing; sing. For it is a new song. It is a song of David. A song of triumph going through out My camp even this night, the enemy is trembling at the new sound that is resonating out of My houses. Oh, such victory. Such Glory! Eye has not seen nor ears heard what is about to happen in My house saith the Father.

For I have spoken of this day in Joel. I have prophesied of this day and this day is upon My church. Surrender to the New Sound. Let it resound throughout the land. Never stop with the New Sound. Just keep rejoicing, saith the Lord.

~~~~~

Much calamity is coming upon America. Much-much calamity is coming and hearts will fail because of fear. Many will run to and fro and they will faint with fear. They have no understanding of this end time event. They have been wondering around in a daze and the truth is not revealed to My people. Therefore the enemy has them for fair game. I warned and I warned, but not all heeded My warnings and now the days of calamity have come upon America. You shall see war on the shores of America. You shall see much blood shed on the shores of America. It will seem like the enemy is triumphing over My people, but if My people will run into the hedge of refuge, I will protect them from all harm. I will provide the way of escape. For this is the hour that I have spoken of in Joel. My Glory shall fall over this land and it shall cover My peoples and a great harvest of souls will be seen throughout the United States of America. Be prepared little one. Be prepared for the great influx of lost and dying souls.

America has not learned to bow her knee to the Living Saviour and therefore she must suffer under the hand of the Almighty One. I **love My** country and therefore I must chastise her and bring her to her knees before the enemy totally destroys her.

Be prepared little one. Be prepared.

~~~~~

Tell My people to humble themselves, fast and pray for direction in the darkness that is coming upon this earth. My people are not prepared for what is coming. Why are they not prepared? Because of the false prophets and false teachers that are preaching peace.

Yes, I have promised peace in the midst of the darkness to My true followers, but the false prophets and false teachers are promising everybody peace in the midst of the storm.

My daughter, when will My church learn the difference between the true and the false?

When will they humble themselves and pray? It is sad to say, but they will only do this as the darkness increases in each of their lives and then there are some that will never learn.

Do I weep over My fallen church? Yes, I do! But I can do nothing about the church. The church must change. The church must seek My face as never before. My church must come to the cross and receive true salvation. I have provided the way, but they must walk in that way.

I **love My** children and I weep over them, just as a true parent weeps over a wayward child.

The after effects of rebellion are more than many will be able to endure, and they will turn away from the cross and follow fables.

Daughter, all must go the way of the cross, for there is no other way.

~ ~ ~ ~ ~

Daniel 10 will confirm what I am about to say to you.

Nation shall rise against nation. My people will suffer much loss because of their complacency. I **love My** people and I watch over them to protect them, but I can only protect those who allow Me to do so.

Much is transpiring in the heavenly realm and soon it shall come down upon this earth.
My church, rise up upon angel wings and transcend all else. For I am about to do a great and mighty thing throughout this land.

My miracle working power is going to be seen all across this great nation. I shall fulfill My promises to My Body of Believers. They shall surely see much angelic activity in their services. They shall know complete abundance in Me. They shall not be led astray as some suppose. I have spoken of the Mighty Miracles that are going to occur and they shall surely come to pass.

Yes, the darkness shall come, because I spoke it. But along with the darkness comes My Glory and My Glory shall invade all darkness.

You shall see many salvations during this time of My Great Visitation. You shall know what it is to see the sick healed. You shall see many raised from the dead. You shall see My Glory manifested all over this land. I will show Myself Mighty to all.

I have been revealing My heart to My prophets and they have been revealing it to the church. Now I will accomplish those things that I have revealed. No more slumbering and sleeping. It is time to work in the harvest field. It is time to bring the harvest in.

In **Daniel 10: 1**; Daniel states: It concerned events certain to happen in the future: times of great tribulation--wars and sorrows, and this time he understood what the vision meant.

God spoke to me about 6 years ago that His Glory was coming. The first day he spoke this to me, His words were: Tell My people that My Glory is coming! Then His very next words were: Daughter, do not grow weary in telling them that My Glory is coming.

In 1980 the Father told me that Great Darkness was coming. It is finally upon us.
We must understand that our Father always forewarns His people of what He is going to do. It is our job to believe His Words, and do not grow weary waiting on them to manifest.

~~~~~

Tell My people that the time is at hand for the signs, wonders and miraculous to occur.

Tell them to build up their most Holy Faith and Step into the Signs, Wonders and Miraculous that stands before them. My people are always waiting for Me to move and I have never stopped moving. In reality, I am waiting for My people to move out into the unknown and do the super miraculous that is already there.

Many are the afflictions of the righteous, but I deliver them out of them all. Tell My people to take their eyes off of their circumstances and place them upon the promises. For My promises are yes and they are amen.

I have a works that must be accomplished (NOW), not sometime down the road. My people must get out of that mentality and step on over into the supernatural.

I **love My** chosen ones and I desire to do great signs and wonders through them, but they will not move out in obedience and faith and just take that first step.

Like I told Peter. Step out of the boat and come into My realm and do not allow the enemy to hold you back any longer. Quit looking around! Just stand on My Word and go forward saith the Father.

I love you little ones and My desire for each one of you is total and complete restoration of all things. Everything the palmer worm and the canker worm has stolen in the past is being restored, even as I speak, to My chosen ones. Do not fret! Do not walk around in discouragement! But look unto Me, the author and finisher of your life. Stay in-tuned to My voice and My voice only and allow Me to take you past all hindrances and allow Me to bring you into the secret chambers of My Heart where I will reveal all things unto You.

NOW! RIGHT NOW is the time of great salvation. Step into My realm and remain there.

LOVE YOU/LOVED YOU…

~~~~~

The hour has come for complete restoration to My Body. The time has come for My people to look up and choose life and not death. The time has come for My Body to receive all the blessings I have promised. It is time to receive all the blessings of Abraham, Isaac and Jacob. It is blessing time church. It is time for you to survive and not go down in complete defeat. I know the enemy has stormed the gates over and over again, but he could not take you out. It has been a hard rough winter, but the winter months have passed and now comes Spring. I **love you** church and I am freely giving in great abundance to all that can believe Me at this given time. Take cover and do not look back. Take cover and come up higher in Me. I am saying take cover, because the enemy would love to uncover My chosen generation, but he cannot. Take cover therefore, and be assured in Me that all is well and all is under control and now it is blessing time once again for My Body of believers.

Tale time to rejoice in Me and then roll over into the new thing that I am accomplishing, even as we speak. You will see the enemy flee on all sides. He will no longer be able to linger at the door and cause the havoc and confusion that he has been causing. His bitter end has come and it its rejoicing time for My Body of believers.

Come on over to the victory side and take the spoils from the enemy. He has been utterly defeated in this great dispensation. Come away My beloved ones and drink of the new wine that I have poured out for My peoples. You are **greatly loved** and you will know without a shadow of a doubt that you are My true beloved ones. History is in the making, even as we speak. The great history of the church that I have been speaking of. Take time right now and rejoice, for I truly am in complete control and the enemy of your soul has been defeated.

~~~~~

Tell My people that I have come after My remnant and I have come to give them strength and power to do the works that I am calling them forth to do. I have prepared a table before them in the presence of their enemies and they shall eat at that table and be filled with fresh manna from their heavenly Father.

Come Church, arise to the call and go forth and do the mighty works that lies before you. I will be with you. I will never leave nor forsake you. I have **loved you** from the beginning of time and I will continue to **love you**. There is so much to be done and so little time to do it.

I have bestowed grace upon you to handle the works I have already called you into. Now, go forth in peace knowing that I am forever with you and I will never leave nor forsake you. You are mine and I am with you.

Even though the enemy rages, I am still more powerful and I am still able to do all that I have spoken.

~~~~~

I am forever with you. I will never leave you nor forsake you. I **love you** so completely. There is not one area of your life that I will not consume with myself, as you draw yourselves unto Me. I am waiting patiently for you, My beloved. I am waiting to encircle you within My loving arms. I am waiting to hold you so close to My bosom, that we become eternally one. I am your all in all. I have given My all just for you. You shall abide under the shadow of the Almighty and no weapon formed against you shall ever prosper. There is no one else for Me, for you are My beloved ones, and I desire to have sweet fellowship with you at all times. There are sweet secrets that I desire to whisper in your ears as we have communion together. How I long to hear your voice daily. How I long for that sweet time of fellowship that I have created you for. Come away with Me this hour My beloved ones and allow Me to take you to a place of sweet essence.

MY LOVE...

~~~~~

My people must know that I Am The Almighty God.

They must know that I am coming in great vengeance upon all those who have rejected Me and My Son. They have also rejected My Holy Spirit.

My love knows no boundaries. And My Wrath knows no end to those of disobedience.

Wake up Body! Wake up and understand that I have spoken and so shall it be. Many are in the bowels of hell cursing Me at this very moment, but they had the same chance that you had and they also refused Me. I have sent My servants into the very throes of hell and brought them back with a message, but even that has not deterred them from their sinful nature.

When is it all going to end? That is a question that so many of the saints are asking? It will end when the Clouds split wide open and My Son returns for the True Church.

Have I not warned that gross darkness was covering the earth and the darkness would become even darker? Is it not happening? Look around about you. What are you hearing? What is happening? Wars and rumor of wars. Mothers and daughters fighting each other. Division between Father and Son. Starvation on every front. Terrorists on every front. It has already started and it is not going to end.

But, I have also promised that I would keep those who were really mine when all this comes to pass. Remnant, hold tight to My hand and do not let go. The enemy will knock at each and every door, but you do not have to open up the door. Hold fast to what you have and watch Me move on your behalf.

~~~~~

I am your Father. I have nourished each one of you from the day you came forth from your mother's womb. I knew all that you were going to do before I ever brought you forth into this world. I know of your failures. I knew of your high times. I knew all about you and I have been ministering **My Love** and My Grace and My Compassion to you. I have been taking your hand; and even pulling you out of the miry clay at times. I have sent My Holy Angels to remove the stumbling blocks that the enemy has placed before your feet. You didn't even know they were there. I have done all this for you for a purpose and that purpose is to have My destiny done here in this earthly realm. I am going to use each and every one of you in the capacity that you were tormented in.

If you were rejected I will send you to the rejected. If you were bound, I am going to send you to those that are bound. Whatever it is you had to go through, that is your area of ministry and I say unto you this night; take My hand totally and completely. Follow Me with all your Spirit; Follow Me with your soul, body and minds. In other words give Me your all today. Leave nothing behind. Give it all to Me and then just follow Me. For I am resurrecting that which was dead and I am bringing new life into that which was dead. I am bringing you all into the fullness of the God-head and you shall have many confrontations with the Most High God. You will each have many angelic visitations, for that is the heritage of the children of the Lord—to walk into the fullness of the God head. And I tell you this day that you will be like My Son Jesus and you will do the great and mighty works that He has done and even greater. You will restore the tabernacle of David. You will rejoice before the King of Kings and Lord of Lords. You will dance and you will sing and you will rejoice for you will finally know who I am; for the Great I Am will give you a face to face revelation.

So I say unto you; rejoice this day; lean not to your own understanding; take My hand totally and completely for I am the only one that can make you survive in this end time calamity that is coming upon this earth and I am not talking about the great tribulation. I am talking about the events that have already begun upon this earth. I am the only one that can make you survive. I am the only one that can keep you safe—safely hidden in My bosom. So take My hand this day and walk with Me totally and completely—100%.

Do not strive with me, just walk with Me. Just hold My hand and let Me lead, guide and direct you.

Quit trying to make your own way. Quit trying to make things happen and just let Me lead guide and direct you. I am your only source of help at this given time. The World System can no longer help you. But I the Lord thy God, I can do all things. I can do all things for you.

The onslaught of the enemy will be great. The death toll will be great; but as you hold My hand you will have everlasting life and you will have it more abundantly than ever before.

Death lies at the door for those who do not serve Him totally and completely—100%. Death lies at the door for the mockers and the scorner and death will consume—death will consume.

~~~~~

Minister love and peace to My people. For peace is where I desire to take My church at this given time. It is mountain climbing time. Just like Moses, I want to take My chosen generation, and this is my chosen generation, I want to take them to the mountain top of total resurrection and love. It is in this mountain top that My people will learn more of Me and begin to understand and know that I am the true God of their salvation.

Teach them of **My Love** that brings a peace that passeth all understanding. It is in Love that perfect peace is manifested. It is in Love that all prayers are fulfilled. It is in Love that they shall see Me in all of My fullness. It is perfect Love that cast out all fear. All fear of the unknown. And I will be taking My people into the regions of the unknown, and from that vantage point, we will win one victory after another.

~~~~~

Tell My people to go to the mountain and stay there in My presence. You are in the time of Moses, where I want to reveal My heart to My people. On the mountain top you will receive divine directions for the future events in this world.

Many are waiting patiently for My voice. But others are getting discouraged and they are starting to walk away, believing in their hearts that I am not going to do the things that I have promised.

I have said before, that your timing is not My timing. Be patient little ones and stand still and watch the salvation of the Lord at work on your behalf. Some have grown bitter and cold from the trials and tribulations that they have had to go through. Some think I am an unjust judge and I am uncaring and unfeeling. But none of this is true. I am working behind the scenes on behalf of those who (truly trust Me.) I will leave no stone unturned. I am going to do just exactly what I HAVE PROMISED THAT I WOULD DO.

Do not jump to conclusions. Stand firm, waiting on My still small voice to lead, guide and direct you in all of your ways. Why be discouraged, when you could be walking in total freedom (in the midst) of your trials. Church, you have (not) learned the valuable lesson of (praise.) As you begin to praise Me, I will remove every mountain. I will bring you up out of every valley. I will overshadow you with **My**

love and My grace and you shall walk in the newness of life that I have promised you.

Come higher Church! Come higher and watch what I am about to do. Take your eyes off of the circumstances. For governments will tumble; the economy will shake; but I am still on the throne. In fact, I would like for you to sit on the throne with Me and view the situations from a heavenly viewpoint, instead of the earthly viewpoint that you refuse to get out of.

Let Me ask you this question? What has all your worrying gotten you? Are you free from your situations? Has the enemy stopped prowling? Come Body! Come higher with Me and allow Me to take you to a place of perfect peace and rest away from all the issues of life that have you weighed down.

I am the Great I Am and I fail you not.

~~~~~

I want you to know Body of Christ that **My Love** for you is unending. I have made a way of escape for each one of you that is holding tightly to My Hand. There is no weapon that has been formed that will in any way bring harm to My chosen ones. There is always a way of correction to any given problem that arises up before you. You are a kingly generation and I have come as the King of Kings and Lord of Lords and I will be your sufficiency.

Take no thought for tomorrow. Today is sufficient unto itself and I am always in total and complete control of all things. A Mighty Outpouring of My Spirit is on the horizon. Do you hear the abundance of rain? The rain is already there. Soak in this outpouring of My Holy Spirit. Revel in My Glory and have no thought of tomorrow. Yes, there will be plenty of opportunities for My Body to be concerned. But I have already spoken (do not be concerned about tomorrow) for I am in total and complete control of tomorrow and surely no weapon formed against you shall prosper.

It is Glory time for My True Followers. Those that have come through the wilderness are now being clothed in white and I assure you that the enemy knows who you are, for he has confronted you on every side and he has tried to destroy you at every port, but to no avail, because (no weapon formed against you could prosper.)

I am laughing in My Heavenly Realm, little ones, for the enemy is defeated. He stands dumfounded, for he just knew you would fall through the cracks as others have done. But not so! Oh, how I am laughing! We have the total victory, little ones. Laugh, Rejoice for your Light has come and it is shining upon you even this very moment.

Hey, church, shout, dance, and rejoice for you have been redeemed from the snare of the fowler. Oh, if you could only see what I see! Oh, if you could only feel what I feel! I cannot contain Myself in this hour. For church, you have surely come through this wilderness experience; this furnace of affliction; this mandate sent out from hell to destroy you at any cost. YOU HAVE COME THROUGH VICTORIOUS.

HEY, SHOUT FOR THE REDEEMED OF THE LORD SAYS SO!

PSALMS 107:1-7 KJV Oh, give thanks to the Lord, for He is good! For His mercy endures forever. Let the redeemed of the Lord say so, Whom He has redeemed from the hand of the enemy, and gathered out of the lands, from the east and from the west, from the north and from the south. They wandered in the wilderness in a desolate way; They found no city to dwell in. Hungry and thirsty, their soul fainted in them. Then they cried out to the Lord in their trouble, and He delivered them out of their distresses. And He led them forth by the right way, that they might go to a city for habitation.

ISAIAH 60:1-3 NKJV Arise, shine; For your light has come! and the glory of the Lord is risen upon you. For behold, the darkness shall cover the earth, and deep darkness the people; but the Lord will arise over you, and His glory will be seen upon you. The Gentiles shall come to your light, and kings to the brightness of your rising.

SONG OF LOVE...

~~~~~

There is coming a day and an hour when My people will rejoice at the sound of My name; for they will surely understand that there is no other name like Mine. I am undergirding My chosen people at this given time and they will bring hope and prosperity to My people. They will walk under an open heaven and they shall carry the glory cloud with them as Moses did and they shall speak words of comfort and hope and they shall rally the people and the peoples will come forth rejoicing and bringing in the sheathes.

They will take comfort in just knowing they are Mine. They will ask for nothing, for they will be content in whatsoever state they are in. This is truly the time of great deliberation for My people.

My chosen people will march to My voice and they shall bring in the lost and dying and they shall minister hope to them in a new way; A way that has not been spoken of before. This is a lost and dying generation; but My chosen will bring that ray of hope that will spark a light and that light will broaden until it consumes the darkness.

The dark spots in this world will be illuminated by this bright light that will emanate from My chosen ones. All will rejoice and be glad. They shall shout; dance and sing for they will know what it is to become free in the presence of the Almighty One of Israel.

Come forward peoples and sing a new song. Sing to the barren desert and watch it blossom and take shape right before your very eyes. I have already sent forth a new song and it has already begun to be sung in My churches. Wherever this new song is sung, prosperity of all kind will spring forth; but this new song must spring forth. It is a song of hope and resurrection power. It is a song of glory, glory, glory. It is a **song of love** abounding. The new sound has begun all across this earth and it will not cease; for the works has already begun to bring in the lost and dying and this is the great harvest that has been prophesied by My Mighty men and woman of valor in My Word.

My light shall surely cover this earth before the great and final day. My son's soon return is being prepared in the heavenly places and He is anxiously awaiting His second return to bring home His bride.

But you must continue to work the works that I have set before you and you must bring in the lost and dying into the house of the Lord.

UNDYING LOVE…

~~~~~

Tell My people that I am coming after them with an **undying love** and I will not relent.

I will bring them into My storehouse of provision and from that place of provision I will supply all of their needs.

I am an all sovereign God and I love My Children and I will not allow them to be tormented and led astray. I have given out many promises and there are still more promises to come. But you must take your stand tonight to stand and when you have done all to stand!

Take heed, lest the enemy get a foothold. Follow strong after My Love and allow Me to love you back in return; for that is the desire of My heart, to shower you with undying love.

UNABASHED LOVE...

~~~~~

Daughter, satan is on the prowl and he is destroying all that he can destroy. It is not make believe, it is real and he is dangerous. He is armed for the kill. If My people do not get down to business; he will take them out one by one. I have already given the mandate to My Holy Angels to go forth with the judgments. I am seeking those who will prepare My people for these judgments.

My people must be told to hold tight to the horn of the altar and not let go at any cost. This is the day of great salvations! This is the day of great floods! Earthquakes and Famines! Please children look up and watch the signs of the times as My Word warns you to do. I am the Alpha, Omega, Beginning and the End. All you that labor come unto Me and I will give you rest. All you who are heavy laden lay that burden at My feet and climb into My arms and allow the peace that passeth all understanding to flood your souls.

Bitter calamity is on all sides, but I have promised to keep My chosen generation in the palm of My hands and I am keeping that promise. No more compromise. No more defending your sins. Let go of all that stains your garments and come let Me wash you white as snow so we can co-labor together.

I have **unabashed love** for My children and I am spreading that love abroad to all that will accept it.

122

I have called so many into My Kingdom Authority, but only a few have been chosen, because so many refused to let go of the things of this world and climb into My lap and allow Me to be their complete sufficiency.

My children, I am calling this night for your undivided attention. I need you to look up and know that your redemption doth draweth nigh. Quit leaning to your own understanding and stand on My Word and My Word only. I will surely bring My Word to pass.

This is the day and the hour of great blessings for those who will walk out of unbelief and truly trust that I will do all that I have said to them. I have given My Children so many promises and they must stand on those promises at this given time and not allow the enemy of their souls to steal, kill and destroy. He is trying to steal the word! He is trying to steal the promises! He is trying to steal your very faith! Look Up! Hold On! For I truly am bringing My Glory Cloud and all things shall transpire before this year comes to an ultimate end.

This is your year of Jubilee. Rejoice! And again I say Rejoice! For I am truly bringing all things to the forefront this year and all will know that I am God. Finally, they shall stop making excuses and they shall say: Surely, this is the Most High God in Action!

Take heed to My voice this night and draw nigh unto Me and do not depart. For I am your safety net at this given time and I will keep you securely in My Pavilion of Safety. Know ye not that I love you? Know ye not that I will never leave thee nor forsake thee? Know ye not from whence you came?

Come now, My little ones, and Rejoice in all your tribulations, for your tribulations shall bring you the total and final victory.

Be not deceived, I am not a man that I should be mocked and I am truly bringing all judgments under My hands.

OVERLAPS – HARVEST/EMBRACE MY LOVE

~~~~~

Church open up your arms wide and receive all that I am about to send into your midst. I am about to unleash My glory in all its abundance and you shall see a great **harvest** of souls begin to come into My houses.

Only those that have love abounding will I use at this given hour. You must not look upon their appearance, but you must look beyond what you see on the outside and allow Me to show you the inside. I am more than enough. I am more than enough. **Embrace Me and My love** and allow Me to shine through you.

It is very vital at this given time that you **embrace My agape love** and then begin to allow it to pour through you to the lost and dying world.

Praise…

1 Chronicles 16:25 KJV

^{25} For great is the LORD, and greatly to be praised: he also is to be feared above all gods...

PRAISE

~~~~~

Tell My people to praise Me from the very depths of their souls. It is time to praise Me for who I am, not what I can give them, but for who I am. Praise Me in the depths of despair. Praise Me when the furnace of affliction has been turned up to its highest. All I desire at this given time is praise. PRAISE ME! PRAISE ME!

Get acquainted with Me through Praise. Learn to dance before the King of Kings and the Lord of Lords. Know Me as the Lover of your souls. Know Me as the eternal one! Come little ones; learn to hear My voice clearer than ever before. Take the first step of intimacy and I will take every step after that. You need more awareness of who I am. You still look at Me as a (far off) Father that does not love His Children. My children, I am just a whisper away. And I listen for every whisper. At the sound of your breath, I respond to My Beloved Ones! Come and fellowship with Me. Come and have sweet communion with your Father. It cost nothing to commune with Me, but it costs everything to (not) commune with Me. I am waiting My Beloved Ones. I am waiting to hear the slightest whisper from your sweet lips.

My Beloved ones please come and commune with Me. I truly do love you. I have waited throughout eternity for this time of sweet fellowship with you.

~~~~~

I am a witness to all the holocaust that is going on across this land. My sons and My daughters, I had to lift My heavy hand and lay it upon America. I have to lay it upon My churches. I have to do this! Because I have to line up with My Word. My Word is True. My Word is Yes and it is Amen. And My Word does not come back to Me void.

Read your word and read it well. All throughout history there has been wars and rumors of wars. There has been destruction on all sides and why? Read My Word. It is all because My People contended with Me. They would not obey, because they contended with Me. They came against Me at every turn. They would not lift their eyes up to Me from whence cometh their help. Instead they clung to their idols. And when I asked them to crush their idols they looked at Me and they laughed and mocked Me to scorn. They kept taking their idols into their hearts.

And I say unto you this night, even those within these walls, there are those in here who still have their idols and you are still bringing them into your hearts; and you will not let go of them; and you will not smash them as I have commanded. Woe be unto those who cling to the idols of this world. Woe be unto those who will not submit all of themselves unto Me even this night. I am a just Father. I must do what I must do. For I am no respecter of persons.

If I would allow you to get away with your sins, then I would have to allow the next one and the next one and the next one. I can't do that My children. I have spoken holiness and holiness it shall be. I have spoken and said there shall be no other Gods before Me. And I tell you this night I demand that I rule and reign within your heart. I am no longer asking! I demand that I rule and reign within your heart! For there will truly be no other Gods before Me. In this dispensation it is Me or it is nothing! I have given you chance after chance, after chance to make Me Lord and what have you done with those chances?

Your praise and worship is beautiful this night. It has come up to the throne as a sweet smelling essence to My nostrils. But I still see the idols in your hearts and they must go. They must go. Do not be partaker of the sin nature. Do not hold onto the hand of Jezebel any longer.

My Children clean up your plate. Clean up your plate before I have to come and clean it up for you. Take My hand. I am lowly in heart. Take My hand and become humble and submissive unto Me. For I am that I am and there is none other like Me

~~~~~

Do you not understand what I am doing oh mighty one? I am the Lord God Jehovah and I fail not. I am preparing a mighty army that will march against the hordes of hell and they will defeat the enemy at every turn.

Take time to praise Me daily, for it is only in your praise that the enemy will flee. It is only in your praise that I will arise upon My Holy Mountain and defeat the enemies of your soul. Why have you forsaken Me oh Jerusalem? Why have you turned your back upon the

Almighty One? What are you doing? Where are you going? You do not understand the vast consequences for your disobedience. You do not understand that the judgment rod is upon you and that you will be consumed by the sword. Turn back! Turn back I say, to the Living God and repent of your wicked evil ways, for I am doing the mighty works that I have been speaking of for years now. No one spared! I will not spare anyone that is not praising Me in their fullness. I will not allow the death angel to pass over those who have flaunted their selves in My face. What kind of God do you truly think that I am? Where do you think I have been while this has been going on? I have been in My Holy Temple watching as My people destroy themselves on all sides. I have been watching as they have trampled on the blood of My precious son Jesus. Do you think that I will allow this to go unpunished? Not So! I have started moving and I am not going to stop. Watch out! Watch your step, for I will not overlook one trespass at this given time, for I have spoken often and asked My people to repent and turn from their wicked evil ways, but to no avail. Now I have no choice, but to march forward and proclaim liberty to those who served Me with all their hearts and bring down the lofty and prideful ones. Sodom and Gomorrah were prideful in their own eyes and they would not relent of their sins, so I had to destroy them. Man can say what they want, but I, The Lord Thy God, I destroyed Sodom and Gomorrah by the hands of My Holy Messengers and I will do the same today.

Cast aside every sin that so easily besets you and lay to waste the things of this world and cling to Me with all your being and allow Me to hide you in My heavenly pavilion while the war rages around about you.

I have spoken of this day and now this day is upon you.

~~~~~

129

From the Potter's Heart

Well, our father is speaking once again and he wants his body to draw close to him in a more intimate way. We can no longer praise him afar off. We must be right in his presence. We must be in the very center of his universe. We must leave this world behind and become like enoch.

We must forsake anything that does not pertain to the heavenly realm. The darkness is getting darker just like our father said it would. There is nothing worth watching on tv. There is nothing worth reading in the paper. It is all gloom, doom and despair. The movies have become nothing but demonic havens to lure the people into the kingdom of darkness.

There isn't one child of god that should be entertaining any of that trash from the throes of hell. Time is being wasted on trash. There is a kingdom works that must be accomplished and we must be about the father's business.

Now is the time! Now is the day of salvation! Now is the time of great resurrection power! Now is the time for god's glory to invade the houses of god. Now is the time of transfering mantles.

Will you be in the right position to receive the mantle that god wants you to have? Only you can answer that question. God has his authors that have written books that he has dictated. It is time for us to read these words from our father and learn kingdom living.

Arise and shine for your light has surely come!

~~~~~

There is yet a short season of infirmities for My Body. But when this is all over, I will already be on the scene, for I have gone before My Body to prepare the way for this great explosion that I have promised years ago. Believe me children, it is coming and it will be very soon and when it comes, you shall have many years of prosperity in Me. By this I mean that I will fill My churches to overflowing. For My signs, wonders and miracles will occur constantly. **All** who seek My face **will** find Me. I will be an everlasting sign to this generation that I am the Great I Am and I fail not.

There has been so much presumption in the body of what they can do and still follow me. Well, I am coming to bring judgment on those who were not and are not following me. I have spoken so many times of My judgment and now it has come. My Body will truly know that I am Lord. Nothing will ever be the same; for I am changing the whole atmosphere in My Churches. You will see all religious spirits die. Only My Holy Spirit will prevail. There will be great gnashing of teeth at this given time; for many will realize that I came and they had no oil in their lamps and the door of opportunity has been shut. Did I not send forth the warning about getting prepared and not to miss out on this next dispensation? I surely did and no one can say I had not spoken before the door closed.

Much admiration for the church is coming on the forefront. People who despised My church will now come forth and praise Me and honor Me in My house of worship. Where the false idols were, they will be no more. For I have come to remove every false idol out of My House. Only My True Spirit will prevail in My Houses of Worship in the coming days.

Censorship:

I will censor what is going on in My house. From this day forward, only My Holy Spirit will prevail in My true churches. It will be line upon line, precept upon precept, here a little and there a little. I will teach My children how to walk in My Spirit, for My Spirit shall fill the tabernacle that praises Me.

I have spoken and so shall it be: There shall be no other god's before Me.

~~~~~

Tell My people that I am on My way. I am not coming, I am on My way. They have long awaited this day and this day has arrived. There is more than enough in My hands for My beloveds. I am bringing blessing after blessing. Did I not promise My church that she would shine in the midst of the storms and tribulations? Well, church, it is time to shine. I say Arise and Shine for your light has come and I am bringing My Glory in an unprecedented way. It will be such an awesome thing, that many will just stand in total amazement at what I am doing. I have given so many promises and the church has been standing on those promises, even when they thought the boat was sinking, they stayed with the boat. Well. church, it is time to receive all the promises that I have spoken. I am not a man that I should lie and I am completing all that I have spoken.

It will be an awesome sight to behold. You have heard my prophets talking about gem stones, well you will also see these gem stones in an unprecedented way. For I am going to allow all My true ones to see these signs, wonders and miracles. Oh, if you could only see right now what I am about to do. You would not be able to contain the shout. You would be shouting from the roof tops. You would be dancing in the streets. But I tell you one thing, you will be dancing. You will dance in My house once again and it will be a sweet dance of praise that will delight My heart. You shall see My Holy Angelic beings walking to and fro through out your sanctuaries. You shall see my angelic beings blessing My people. It shall be a sight to behold and there will be nothing like it ever again. For this is the final thrust of the super natural and I have waited a long time to bring this to My chosen generation of faithful ones.

~~~~~

There is a place in My Kingdom for those who are obedient, but all others will be cast out. I am taking My Chosen Ones to a place of refuge from the storms that are brewing on the horizon. All of My children must walk under the Shadow of the Almighty, for perilous times are before them.

I have so much to do and so little time to get it accomplished. My forerunners are growing battle weary, but I have sent My Holy Angels to strengthen them to go forward and complete the works I have started.

Many false prophets have emerged out of nowhere and My people must discern what is truth and what is false. Take heed to what you hear. Test the spirits, for they will come as angels of light and they will deceive many.

Tomorrow is always a new dawning and when life seems too hard to bear, just look up and praise Me, for I am surely in the midst of your praises. I have raised up a new standard all across this land and I expect My chosen ones to walk in purity of heart as well as mind, soul and spirit. Do not allow the enemy to take you off course at this given time, for he is out to deceive even the very elect.

You need not strive for revenge. I the Lord Your God, I will repay the fowler for all that he has done to My elect. I have called you forth as Paul to do a mighty works on My behalf, now be courageous and go forth knowing that your Father who sends you forth is able to keep you in the midst of a perverse generation. And this generation is perverse. It is worse than Sodom and Gomorrah. Children, do not seek your own pleasures, but seek ye first the Kingdom of Heaven and all else will be added unto you.

Rejoice in Me and know that I am about My business. And My business is all about building My Kingdom, not the kingdoms of this world.

~~~~~

Arise and shine, for your light has come! It is time to come out of darkness and come into the glorious light. It is time church to abide under the shadow of the Almighty and never look back ever again. It is time to put on the full armor of God and arise above your circumstances.

If you do not do this, the enemy is going to take you totally out of My presence. There are too many of My children going the way of Baal daily, thinking they can still make heaven their home. Do not be deceived church, do not be deceived. You cannot serve Me and Baal. You have to choose.

The hour is slipping away when you can repent and turn back to Me, the true and living God. Do not miss your door of opportunity. Take up your cross immediately and follow Me with all of your heart.

The enemy has begun to place old circumstances back into your path, to draw you away from your destiny and to draw you into the very throes of hell. Perdition is waiting anxiously for My children. What are you going to choose to do little ones? What are you going to choose to do? Do not miss your open door, for I am already closing this door.

Church, do you not understand that I am withdrawing My Holy Spirit from your presence? I will no longer allow you to trample My precious Holy Spirit under your feet. You will no longer come into My House and praise Me and then go out into the world and be just like the world. I have called My church to be separate from the world. I have called you to be a peculiar people. And all you do is shatter My image daily. The world doesn't want Me, because you portray Me as a God of confusion. The world is already confused. They want the truth. They want freedom from their bondages. They need the Holy Spirit to indwell in them and lead, guide and direct them.

Where are you at church? Why are you not about the Father's business? I am calling, are you listening?

Matthew 11:15 NKJV (He who has an ear let him hear.)

Revelation 2:7 NKJV (7. "He who has an ear, let him hear what the Spirit says to the churches. To him who overcomes I will give to eat from the tree of life, which is in the midst of the Paradise of God.")

Isaiah 60:1 - 3 Arise, shine; For your light has come! And the glory of the Lord is risen upon you. For behold, the darkness shall cover the earth, and deep darkness the people; but the Lord will arise over you, and His glory will be seen upon you. The Gentiles shall come to your light, and kings to the brightness of your rising.

~~~~~

This is not the time for retreat. This is the time to go forward like never before. There are no limitations to the children of God; for the heavens are open wide over them and they shall walk in the fullness of the open heavens at this given time.

Praise will increase to a degree that all will surrender all to Me and they shall lay their lives at My feet and they shall not go back; for they will understand that there is absolutely nothing to go back to.

Daughter, admonish My people to smile and go forth with a new song in their hearts and on their lips, for I truly have manifested My Glory already and it is going to explode into a mighty outpouring of My heavenly gifts and many signs, wonders and miracles shall be seen all across this land.

It is explosion time and I am about to explode all across this nation. Those who would not bow their knees will bow because of the heaviness of My Glory.

Transformation after transformation shall occur. The mighty miracles that I have been talking about will be seen by all. Some will still shun My Glory, but that is OK. I want My true people to just keep marching and never look back.

A great and mighty earthquake is about to hit this land and through this earthquake many souls will be saved.

Get ready church, for the mighty influx of people that I am sending your way; for I have spoken much through My prophets and I will perform every word that I have spoken.

~~~~~

This is the hour of great deception in the land as well as in the church. I will not compromise My Word. My Word is yes and it is Amen. Man must change, for I will not. Truth is truth and My Word is nothing but truth. Children; raise your standards, because I am not going to lower mine. Take your seat in the heavenly places with Me and allow Me to bring you forth in total humility and obedience to My Will for your lives and this world.

I am your mainstay, not man or the world systems. I will lead, guide and direct your footsteps and when I lead, guide and direct your footsteps, you will walk in the fullness of who I am and who you have become because of Me.

Do not stay outside the Holy of Holies but come into the center of the Holy of Holies and sup and dine with me continually from this moment forth. I am that I am and I do not change.

There is coming a day of great praise and jubilation for all those who have kept their standards high, for I am about to reward those who would not compromise. I am about to pour out Myself unto My peoples like never before and there will be a landslide of souls being brought into My Kingdom.

Today is the day of great salvations. Today is the day of great rejoicing before the King of Kings and Lord of Lords. Today Is The

Day! Not tomorrow, but today! So rejoice in Me and know that I Am is in control of all things in your life and in the lives of those around about you.

~~~~~

My children, it has been a long and arduous battle, but the time of rest is upon you. You must take time and rest totally and completely in My presence. You must take time and rest, for the warfare is going to thicken and there will be other battles to fight, but for now, just rest at My feet and be refreshed for the brand new battle that lies before you.

Children, why do you get so perplexed at all the battles you have to fight? Study My Word. Did not My children fight battle after battle, but was I not there for them winning every battle. Study Joshua. What did I do for him at the battle of Jericho? Study David. What did I do for David? Come up higher children. Learn to praise and adore Me and you will not be afraid of the battles, but you will be like David when he fought Goliath. You will volunteer for the next battle, for you will know that the Lord thy God is fighting the battle for you.

> **Psalm 3: 1 – 8 TLB** 1. O Lord, so many are against me.
> So many seek to harm me. I have so many enemies. 2.
> So many say that God will never help me. 3. But Lord, you
> are my shield, my glory, and my only hope. You alone can
> lift my head, now bowed in shame. 4. I cried out to the
> Lord, and He heard me from His temple in Jerusalem.
>
> 5. Then I lay down and slept in peace and woke up safely,
> for the Lord was watching over me. 6. And now,
> although ten thousand enemies surround me on every side,
> I am not afraid. 7. I will cry to Him, "Arise, O Lord!

Save me, O my God!" And He will slap them in the face, insulting them and breaking off their teeth.8. For salvation comes from God. what joys He gives to all His people.

WORSHIP

~~~~~

I was dressing this morning and started to cry uncontrollably. I came into the computer room and started crying out to God and this is what I heard:

My heart weeps for My house, for My house will not hear My pleas for repentance. My sorrow goes so deep. My heart breaks at every turn. Why children? Why won't you turn to Me with your whole heart? Why does the world have such a pull upon you and your families? I have pondered over this for ages, and I have only one answer. The world holds more for your heart than I do, so you think!

The wages of war are so costly. But the wars must come now, for My people would not repent and turn from their wicked evil ways. These wars will cost you more than you care to pay. There will be great wailing and gnashing of teeth heard on the streets. For the soon coming despair will outweigh anything that the world has ever experienced. Many will bemoan the very day they were born. The homosexual community will be destroyed. I will not be mocked. I am not a bastard. I am the true Father of all creation. Why do you, church, think the enemy created? Why do you think he is in control? You will soon see who is in control, and for some it will be too late, for others, they will finally see that all I have spoken is coming to pass and they will fall upon their faces in total worship of a loving and caring Father.

Hold tight to what you have in Me, church! Hold tight, for it will be worth it all in the very end.

Much destruction on all sides. Many will be running to and fro, and many will be seeking places of refuge, but will be unable to find any. Total disaster awaits this world as you see it. I am not a God of destruction, but I do destroy when necessary. As you read My Word, you will see destruction after destruction and devastation on all sides. This was because My people refused to follow My voice. I sent My Son, so His blood would be an atonement for sins, but even that has been trampled under foot. I am left with no alternative, but to bring destruction, so I can rebuild My world once again.

Woe upon woe. Sorrow on all sides. But I will be with My remnant in all this. You who have chosen Me in the years past have chosen a good thing, all those who chose the things of the world will reap what they have sown. Go church and preach My gospel to a lost and dying world. For My Son will soon return for a glorious church, one without spot nor wrinkle.

I ask you to abide under the shadow of the Almighty until My Son's soon return.

~~~~~

This is a brand new generation of believers. They are not like the old generation of believers who hear and do not perceive. This new generation will bite into My word and devour it in an instant. They shall know their God like no others have known Me. They will not bite and devour one another. They will be united in one heart and one mind and one spirit and they shall walk in total unity and accomplish what no other generation has ever accomplished.

A new breed of hound dogs! They will sniff out the enemy at every turn. They will rout him out and totally destroy him and all his cohorts. You will see a mass slaughter of the kingdom of darkness with this new breed that has come upon the scene. Get ready for the great landslide of souls. For the new breed will bring in the lost and the dying. They will have faith in their God to deliver to the utmost all who are lost and dying.

Great rejoicing in the heavenly camp! Great exuberation at this given time! The Holy Angels are standing at alert, awaiting the commands of My people to send them forth to do warfare for them. Victory after Victory after Victory. Rejoicing! Dancing like David Danced! Singing and praising will be heard in the streets, for My people are being rejuvenated even as I speak and they shall come forth singing and dancing with all of their hearts and they will **worship** the King of Kings and the Lord of Lords at this given time.

~~~~~

The great slaughter has begun. The slaughtering of My peoples. The ones who would not heed My warnings of great destruction coming across this land. The deception is running rampant in My Body of Believers.

My church that has heeded My voice will rise to a higher height in Me. They shall be able to hear My Audible Voice as I speak great instructions for this end-time time table.

They shall walk under an anointing that will not stop. This time, the revival fires will not grow dim. For My true peoples are going to be set on fire with My Glory and they shall encompass this vast universe with Great signs and wonders following where ever they go.

Teachers of My Word will rise to a new height of understanding of My Gospel and they shall preach under a heavy anointing and all shall understand what they are saying, for the anointing shall break every yoke of bondage and the ears will pop open and they will be able to hear clearly what thus saith the Lord God Almighty from his heavenly throne room, where I am surrounded by My Heavenly Host of Angelic beings. These angelic beings shall be sent to earth to manifest My Glory for My true believers. This angelic host shall once again fulfill My Word. Read what My angelic host accomplished for My true believers.

Riches upon riches have been laid up in heaven for My chosen generation. You shall see the yokes of bondage being broken off of My true peoples and you shall see them set perfectly free.

Rejoice chosen ones. Rejoice, for your time to arise and shine has come upon you and you shall accomplish all that I am sending you forth to accomplish. No more back sliding. No more compromising My word. Just total victory on all sides! Just total restoration on all fronts! The time has come and now is when My true children will worship Me in Spirit and in Truth.

Do you feel the electricity in the atmosphere? Do you feel the anticipation of My Heavenly Hosts as they stand ready to go forth and do My biding upon this earth?

Rejoice My chosen ones. Really Rejoice, for Victory has already come into your camps and the enemy of your souls has been completely broken. You are free! You are free! You are free! Walk in liberty, for you are truly free from the snare of the fowler, never to be bound up again. You Are Free. Can you hear Me shouting this across the Heavenly atmosphere. My voice is resounding all across the

Heavenlies. You Are Free. Rejoice. And again I say Rejoice forever more, for I have come and there is none other like unto Me. I am that I am and I have come upon the scene with all of My Glory. Now, just Rejoice and watch the salvation of the Lord at work on your behalf.

As God was giving this last paragraph, I could feel the excitement in his voice. I could feel the great swelling love and the rejoicing that is already taking place in the heavenlies. Peoples, we are there, all we have to do is walk in it.

~~~~~

How the heathen do rage. They are howling from every corner of the earth. They are raising up the banners of the wicked one and they are demanding their rights. They are demanding that they be heard above the roar of the Glory. But they will not be heard. They will not get their rights. But they will get what I have in store for them, eternal judgment and damnation. I have already tried the heathen and found them wanting. They are a generation of evil doers that will not repent nor hold their peace. They are demanding; greedy; unrestrained evil ones that have not the knowledge of Christ. They have hardened their hearts to the point of total damnation. Oh, how the heathen do rage. But My Glory shall shine upon My True Church during this time of gross darkness. My Glory shall surely come upon this dark land and it shall bring forth My Light in an unprecedented way. Many will fall down and worship the King of Kings but there are many that will maintain their stance of damnation, for they have hardened their hearts and cannot come forth into the full knowledge of who I am.

My light shall never stop shining, for it shall cover this earth and then My Son shall return for his bride and then the end shall surely come.

~~~~~

Yes, tell My Body of Believers that I am about to come in an unprecedented way. I shall tower over all the darkness that looms upon this earth and by My Mighty Power; I shall cause My Glory to prevail over this darkness. My true bride is coming forth full of My Glory to penetrate the gross darkness that has covered this earth in a prevalent way. No matter what the world thinks, I am still in total and complete control of all things and I am about My business of cleaning up My Body of Believers.

Scam after scam has prevailed all across this nation, but I the Lord thy God, I am prevailing in the midst of this adversity. I am sending My Holy Light to shine upon a perverse generation of young people and you shall see them emerge into this glorious light and do great and mighty exploits for the King of Kings and Lord of Lords.

Keep your eyes upon the youth church. Keep your eyes upon the youth, for they are coming and they shall worship Me in Truth and in Spirit and they shall know their God supplies.

~~~~~

Utter chaos all over this land. My people have still not chosen me as their Lord and Savior. They are still looking to flesh and blood to bring them through. All flesh and blood will do is sink them further into the miry clay. When oh when will they ever learn to repent and turn from their wicked evil ways?

I spoke about the false prophets and they are already on the land and the peoples are listening to them and they are obeying what they are saying. When will they learn to hear My voice and only My voice? Sin is running rampant and the peoples are saying who cares what your God says? Daughter, they will soon learn what your God has to say, for your God is turning the tables on this wicked evil generation. This generation that has no restraint. This generation that goes after evil continually. Where will it all end you ask? In the pits of hell little one; in the pits of hell.

I have surely spread a table for My true worshipers in the presence of their enemies and you shall surely see your enemies under your feet shortly. My true saints will see victory on every side and they shall be the head and not the tail.

Many false witnesses have also come on the scene, claiming to walk in my supernatural powers and they are walking in their own powers. They do not know Me and they do not know My ways. But My true church is arising and My true church will being forth the truth and the truth shall set the captives free.

I have spoken so many things over this generation and it shall surely come to pass. Just stand aside and allow the maker of this universe have his way.

OVERLAPS HOLY/WORSHIP

~~~~~

Follow your heart in all things, for I am in the heart. I am leading My people down a path of great adventures and they will once again understand that I truly am Lord of this nation. They will understand that I do things in My timing and not theirs. I have not missed anything. After all, am I not the creator of all things? Therefore, I know the perfect timing of all things.

Daughter, tell My peoples to look up, for their redemption doth draweth nigh. I am their redemption and I am coming in a Great Cloud of Glory. But before that eventful day occurs, there is so much work to be done here on this earth for My Kingdom. Many souls to be brought into the Kingdom. Many have not even heard the gospel of Jesus Christ. Many have not had the opportunity to receive My Son into their bosoms. So many souls hanging in the balance and no one to speak the truth to them; to allow them to decide their fate. I want every man to have the opportunity to receive My Son or reject Him. I want no one to perish. I am making a way for the Word to go forth, and I need dedicated committed servants to go forth with this gospel that saves the souls from eternal damnation.

Rise up peoples of this nation and tune your ears to My voice, for I am speaking volumes, but not many are listening. I am calling from the four corners of this earth, calling all who will heed the sound of My voice.

So much idolatry out there. So much walking in the flesh, leaving My Holy Spirit out of their lives and then blaming Me when all things tumble around about them.

Hold up Holy hands and worship Me with a pure heart and then I will come and sup with you. Then I will speak softly into your ears the plans that I have for this nation. Plans that will edify and lift up. Plans to bring this nation to her knees and then rise her back up again.

Come My Holy Vessels. Come unto Me with pure hearts; pure motives and pure hands and I will send you to the nations with a Right Now Word to give to My people who sit in My houses all over this nation and are perishing.

OVERLAPS – PRAISE/EVERLASTING
LOVE/LOVE ME

~~~~~

Tell My children that I am with them wither so ever they go. Tell My children that **I love them** with an **everlasting love**. Tell them to prepare their selves for a mighty move of My spirit. I am coming on the waves of love and I am going to restore and refresh My Body. The battle has been long and bloody, but My true soldiers have endured the good fight of faith and have come forth victoriously.

A great landslide of souls is coming into the Body of Christ. Many salvations are riding on the wings of My Spirit. The church will grow from this moment forth and you shall see great rejoicing in My Body of Believers.

They are learning how to **praise** Me through all their troubles. They are learning to **praise** Me when they don't feel like praising. They are finally learning what it means to truly praise the living Father.

~~~~~

The atmosphere is becoming cloudier and cloudier. There is much deception going on in this United States. The government is so corrupt and the politicians are covering up so much debris. But watch what I am going to do. Watch and see what is going to transpire over the next two months of 2009. I am bringing My People to a total resting place in Me and they shall know Me as a triune God. They shall know Me as their Everlasting Father. They shall see Me face to face once again. Once again they shall stand on the precipice of Joy unspeakable and full of Glory. They will not be concerned about the persecution that rages around about them, for they shall be totally full of My Glory continually and they will have died out to flesh and they will stand for the sure words of My Word.

Daughter, there is going to be such a glorious time upon this earth. Great signs wonders and miracles will be manifested by those who truly **love Me** with all of their hearts. They will know what it is that they are working for at last and they will do it with gladness of heart. The enemy will be uprooted at every turn. True happiness once again shall prevail. My people will become another Paul; Peter; Isaiah and Moses. You shall see little one, you shall surely see Me manifest Myself amongst My peoples that are called by my name.

Rejoice; rejoice; for Rejoicing time is in the house. Sing **praises** unto Me, the King of Glory. Sing **praises** unto Me out of a heart of Joy unspeakable and full of glory. Sing; sing; sing. For it is a new song. It is a song of David. A song of triumph going through out My camp even this night, the enemy is trembling at the new sound that is resonating out of My houses. Oh, such victory. Such Glory! Eye has not seen nor ears heard what is about to happen in My house saith the Father.

For I have spoken of this day in Joel. I have prophesied of this day and this day is upon My church. Surrender to the New Sound. Let it resound throughout the land. Never stop with the New Sound. Just keep rejoicing, saith the Lord.

CONCLUSION...

Ecclesiastes 12: 1 KJV

[1] Remember now thy Creator in the days of thy youth,
while the evil days come not...

CONCLUSION

Jesus is the Spirit of Prophecy. When you serve the Father there is no information that He will withhold from you. This is why as you serve Him He will open up your heart and cause you to receive from Him. This is the dispensation of the God speaking to His people. His desire is towards us and the more that we learn to hear His voice the better off the Body of Christ will be.

It is my hope that as you read through that you learned about our Father. In these days you must have an intimate relationship with Him if you expect to make it through the gross darkness that is coming upon the land. You are apart of the Remnant. Those who have been hand picked by God to work for Him and carry His glory.

There is no good thing that the Father will withhold from you. Because you have set your love upon Him, because you have set your hand to the plow to bring in the harvest you will find a greater sense of His grace and His love flowing through you.

May you be blessed in all that you endeavor to do for the Father.

Barbara Lynch, Reverend

The Lighthouse Inc., Church.

The Father has chosen her to be an Evangelist, Revivalist and Glory Carrier for Him. Her heart's desire is to please her Father in Heaven. She is committed to staying before Him and seeking His face at every moment.

Pst. Barbara walks under many anointings and has carried forth and completed many assignments for the Lord. No stranger to pain and suffering herself, Pst. Barbara has a heart for children and those who are down and out. She has compassion for the lost and dying of this world and she loves to minister to God's people. She practices love at every level and teaches others to do the same.

It is in service to God's people; ministering, mentoring, leading and encouraging them to seek the deeper depths of the Father that she allows the Father to use her with complete abandon. Selfless, caring, willing to go to any length to reach the hearts of the Father's people, she has laid her life down for Jesus, her true friend.

The Holy Spirit would teach her everything that she would need to know. The Father led Pst. Barbara to open a Church called "Haven of Rest" in her home in

1984. As the Fathers plans grew, and the Father expanded the ministry from "Haven of Rest" to the "Lighthouse Church Inc". in 1991. She has been instrumental in fulfilling the call to equip the Saints of God to do the work of the Father. Because she allowed the Father to train her in His ways she has led many to His throne of Grace.

She is mentoring those who have a heart to be in the ministry. She is a forerunner. Pst. Barbara has a powerful deliverance ministry where many captives are being set free. She is actively working to set God's people free through deliverance. Pst. Barbara leads a small band of committed warriors who love the Lord. She is committed to teaching and training the Body of Christ to walk in the gifts of the Spirit.

As the Father leads Pst. Barbara is accepting speaking engagements. For more information call (302) 697-1472. She is located at 6 South Railroad Avenue; Wyoming, DE 19934-1026. You may follow her ministry at www.lighthousechurchinc.org